DATE DUE

			PRINTED IN U.S.A.

EXPLORING THE ANCIENT
AND MEDIEVAL WORLDS

First Peoples of the Americas and the European Age of Exploration

Patricia Dawson

Cavendish
Square

New York

Published in 2016 by Cavendish Square Publishing, LLC
243 5th Avenue, Suite 136, New York, NY 10016

Website: cavendishsq.com

This publication represents the opinions and views of the author based on his or her personal experience, knowledge, and
research. The information in this book serves as a general guide only. The author and publisher have used their best efforts
in preparing this book and disclaim liability rising directly or indirectly from the use and application of this book.

CPSIA Compliance Information: Batch #WS15CSQ

All websites were available and accurate when this book was sent to press.

Library of Congress Cataloging-in-Publication Data

Dawson, Patricia (Patricia Adelaide)
First peoples of the Americas and the European age of exploration / Patricia Dawson.
pages cm. — (Exploring the ancient and medieval worlds)
Includes bibliographical references and index.
ISBN 978-1-50260-685-3 (hardcover) ISBN 978-1-50260-686-0 (ebook)
1. Indians of North America—Juvenile literature. 2. Indians of Central America—Juvenile literature.
3. Indians of South America—Juvenile literature. 4. America—Discovery and exploration—European—Juvenile literature.
5. Discoveries in geography—History—Juvenile literature. I. Title.

E77.4.D39 2016
970.004'97—dc23

2015014687

Editorial Director: David McNamara
Editor: Nathan Heidelberger
Copy Editor: Regina Murrell
Art Director: Jeff Talbot
Designer: Amy Greenan
Senior Production Manager: Jennifer Ryder-Talbot
Production Editor: Renni Johnson
Photo Research: J8 Media

Printed in the United States of America

Contents

The Pyramid of the Sun was the largest building in the city of Teotihuacán, which flourished during the Classic period of pre-Columbian history.

CHAPTER ONE
The Pre-Columbian World

Historians use the term **pre-Columbian** to refer to the numerous cultures that thrived in the Americas before **Christopher Columbus** reached the continents in 1492 CE, setting off a wave of European exploration, conquest, and exploitation of the **New World**. While the term is sometimes used in connection with the early native peoples of North America, it is more conventionally applied only to those cultures that were based in present-day Central and South America. Sadly, these once great civilizations are no more. They were nearly all destroyed within a hundred years of Columbus's momentous arrival.

In Central America, the greatest pre-Columbian cultures were those of the **Aztecs** and the **Maya**; also significant were the **Olmecs**, the Tarascans, the **Toltecs**, the **Zapotecs**, and the citizens of **Teotihuacán**. In South America, the principal civilization of the pre-Columbian period was that of the **Incas**; other important cultures were those of the Chibcha, the **Mixtecs**, and the Mochica.

Although the civilizations of Central America and South America developed largely in isolation, they had either a common heritage or sufficient contact with each other to share several characteristics and practices, notably (but by no means exclusively) in matters of religion. Several of them also used similar methods for calculating time on the basis of a 260-day year.

The Aztecs and the Maya were technologically adept people whose civil engineering skills enabled them to achieve some of the world's greatest architectural feats. The many temples at Teotihuacán, Tikal, Palenque, El Mirador, and Copán can still be seen today and attest to the remarkable skills of their builders. In addition, their sculpture, jewelry, pottery, and textiles are evidence of highly sophisticated craftspeople. The Incas were equally accomplished, as evidenced by the remains of their settlements at **Machu Picchu** and Cuzco.

Eventually, however, the very isolation of these civilizations was a contributing factor in their downfall. When the Europeans arrived in the fifteenth century CE, they brought with them deadly diseases, to which the indigenous peoples had no immunity. They quickly succumbed and died by the thousands.

Common Characteristics

It is generally assumed that the first inhabitants of Central America and South America were groups of Asiatic hunters who entered the region from North America. Originally, they probably came from Siberia, traveling across the land that connected Asia and North America before sea levels rose and formed the modern Bering Strait. The earliest archaeological remnants found for pre-Columbian settlements in Central America and South America date from around 17,000 BCE.

Gradually, many of the previously nomadic peoples settled in particular locations. They adapted well to the enormously varied terrains of the region, which ranged from desert to jungle and from lowlands to some of the highest mountain ranges in the world.

All the pre-Columbian cultures were based on agriculture. Remarkably, only the Incas had a beast of burden—the llama. The peoples of the other civilizations transported almost everything on their own backs. The tool technology of most of these cultures was limited, despite their great achievements in crafts and architecture. Simple hoes were used by the Aztecs and the Maya for building terraces, draining swamps, and irrigating land. Some of the terraces built by the Incas can still be seen on the mountains around Cuzco.

Although the peoples of the pre-Columbian cultures used the wheel to make models and toys, they did not use it for transportation or any other practical purpose. Their earliest buildings were probably

Regions and Epochs of Pre-Columbian Society

For ease of reference, historians have divided the pre-Columbian cultures into three periods: the **Preclassic** (circa 1500 BCE–300 CE), the **Classic** (ca. 300–900 CE), and the **Postclassic** (ca. 900–1540 CE).

The area occupied by pre-Columbian cultures has been divided into three clearly defined regions: the **Mesoamerican** area, the Intermediate area, and the Central Andean area. The Mesoamerican area comprises present-day Mexico and the Central American countries of Belize, Guatemala, Honduras, and El Salvador. The Intermediate area covers the present-day Central American countries of Nicaragua, Costa Rica, and Panama, together with the South American countries of Colombia, Venezuela, and Ecuador. The Central Andean area includes present-day Peru, Bolivia, and northern Chile.

made of wood or of woven or bundled fiber; later buildings were made of **adobe** or great blocks of stone, which were maneuvered into position on wooden rollers. The stones were cut and ground to fit together perfectly without the use of mortar.

Using only these basic techniques, the peoples of the Central Andean area (modern Peru, Bolivia, and northern Chile) and Mesoamerica (modern Mexico, Belize, Guatemala, Honduras, and El Salvador) built platform temples, pyramids, palaces, and tombs, many of which can still be seen today. The pyramids may occasionally have been used as tombs, but according to surviving records, they were constructed primarily for political and ceremonial purposes. The records were written in pictographs on deer parchment or bark cloth.

Throughout Central America and South America, the pre-Columbians excelled in many forms of arts and crafts. They carved stone sculptures (mainly in Mesoamerica), modeled clay figurines, and produced pottery cups and vases. They decorated their utensils and sometimes their buildings with incised carvings, molded designs, and painted scenes. While painting was common to all these peoples, it was the Aztecs, the Maya, and the Mixtecs who developed forms of writing.

La Mojarra Stela 1, which has been dated to 159 CE, is the oldest known example of decipherable writing found in the Americas.

Pre-Columbian metalsmiths worked with gold, silver, and copper (including tumbaga, an alloy of copper and gold) as early as 1200 BCE in the Central Andean area and by around 800 CE in Mesoamerica and the Intermediate area (modern Nicaragua, Costa Rica, Panama, Colombia, Venezuela, and Ecuador). They alloyed bronze around 1200 CE and soon learned to cast metal by the lost-wax process (see sidebar, page 12). They also learned how to solder metal and developed methods for embossing, gilding, engraving, and inlaying it.

Pre-Columbians wove textiles from cotton and wool, and they painted, stamped, and embroidered designs on the fabric. Many of these textiles were prized more highly than gold, and some of the most valuable fabrics were reserved for ceremonial purposes.

The Olmec Civilization

By around 1500 BCE, many of the formerly nomadic groups in Central America and South America had developed great civilizations. This was the start of the era now known as the Preclassic period, which continued until around 300 CE.

The earliest pre-Columbian culture—that of the Olmecs—emerged on the coast of the Gulf of Mexico. By 600 BCE, the Olmecs

Pre-Columbian Writing

In 1988 CE, a team of US academics deciphered two-thirds of the text inscribed on a basalt **stela** (commemorative pillar) that was unearthed two years earlier near Veracruz, Mexico.

Originally carved by the Olmec people in 159 CE (the exact year was established by carbon-dating methods), the stela was 6 feet (1.6 meters) long and 4 feet (1.2 m) wide. It bore the image of a man in a headdress. Around this central figure were 21 columns of **hieroglyphic** writing comprising 150 **logograms**. A logogram is a picture that represents a word; examples in English include the ampersand (&), which represents the word "and."

The Olmec logograms were found to represent a warrior king, a jaguar, the sunrise, stars, and a fertility symbol; together, they referred to a renewal ceremony. While older examples of writing have been discovered elsewhere in the Mesoamerican region, their meanings have yet to be deciphered. This stela thus represents the oldest piece of comprehensible writing found to date in the Americas.

had developed a social and economic system that extended westward and southward to outlying settlements. Their three major ceremonial centers—known as the heartland—were San Lorenzo, La Venta, and Tres Zapotes.

San Lorenzo, the first to be built, flourished from the twelfth century BCE until around 900 BCE, when it was destroyed. It was replaced by La Venta, which was built on a large island (surrounded by a swamp) to the northeast of San Lorenzo. The central complex of La Venta featured a large pyramid that was 100 feet (30 m) tall and surrounded by platform temples and plazas all laid out in a symmetrical plan based on an axis determined by astrology.

The Olmecs are known today for the massive stone heads they left behind.

The Olmec pyramids were built primarily of clay, although the pavements and drainage systems may have been made of stone. The Olmecs carved huge heads, 8–12 feet (2.4–3.1 m) tall, out of basalt. These gigantic stone sculptures may have been portraits of rulers. The Olmecs also carved jade to create figurines, masks, pendants, and containers. Other Olmec monuments depicted important events with pictographs. The curvilinear art style of the Olmecs was reproduced in cave paintings and in reliefs carved into the walls of caves. Jaguars with human features and humans with jaguar aspects were recurrent motifs in Olmec art.

Around 400 BCE, La Venta was destroyed and replaced by Tres Zapotes, around 100 miles (160 kilometers) to the northwest. By this time, however, the Olmec civilization was in decline. At its peak, the Olmec population probably had thirty-five thousand people. The Olmec social system was hierarchical, with priests and nobles at the top, merchants and craftsmen in the middle, and farmers and peasants at the bottom.

Unlike the Olmec culture, the Colima, Jalisco, Guerrero, and Nayarit cultures (named after the modern Mexican states in which the ancient sites were discovered by archaeologists) are notable for their clay work, effigy pots, and figurines rather than for their architecture. In Guerrero, however, some small replicas of temples and altars, carved in stone, have been discovered.

The City of Teotihuacán

The Preclassic era of pre-Columbian civilization was followed by the Classic period, which is generally dated from around 300 CE to 900 CE. The earliest archaeological remains from this period come from Teotihuacán (the name means "place of the gods"), a city-state that developed in a valley around 25 miles (40 km) northeast of present-day Mexico City. First settled around 600 BCE, Teotihuacán had become the sixth largest city in the world by around 600 CE, covering an area of approximately 8 square miles (20 square kilometers) and having a population of approximately two hundred thousand people. Most of its temples and residential buildings were destroyed by fire around 750 CE.

Teotihuacán was laid out on a grid system. A major avenue, the Street of the Dead, ran through its center, and there was a large complex of religious and other important buildings at the northern end of the avenue. To the east of the avenue lay the Pyramid of the Sun, the largest building in the city. The walls of the temples and palaces were covered with murals. In the Tepantitla Palace, one mural

This reproduction of a mural from the Tepantitla Palace at Teotihuacán shows Tlalocan, the water goddess. The palace walls were decorated with many similar murals.

Lost-Wax Casting

The metalsmiths of the pre-Columbian era were ingenious and skilled craftsmen who learned to cast sculptures in metal using the lost-wax process.

The method worked as follows: First, the craftsmen fashioned in wax a model of the sculpture to be cast. They then surrounded the wax model with a layer of clay, leaving a few holes in the clay. The clay was then baked in a hot oven until it set hard. During the baking process, the wax melted and ran out through the holes, leaving a hollow clay mold. The clay mold was then placed in a bed of sand, and hot molten metal was poured into it. When the metal had cooled and solidified, the completed metal sculpture was removed from its casing by breaking the clay mold.

depicts Tlalocan (the water goddess) with her hands outstretched and water flowing through her fingers. Plants and wildlife grow from her head, and all around her are fertility symbols. The murals reveal little about the rulers of Teotihuacán; it may be that the area was governed by an elite body of several people rather than by a single monarch. It is notable that the paintings do not contain any scenes of human sacrifice, war, or battles.

The Teotihuacáns mined **obsidian** (a glassy volcanic rock) from nearby mines and used it to make cutting tools, which they traded for other goods. Merchants from Teotihuacán traveled many hundreds of miles to trade, and the city itself was a flourishing commercial center. Among the numerous artifacts created at Teotihuacán were stone masks, jade and serpentine figures, and fine ceramic orangeware vessels.

Most of the citizens of Teotihuacán lived in apartment compounds built out of locally quarried limestone and surrounded by high walls.

The apartments were single-story buildings, and one apartment might consist of several rooms. Cooking was carried out indoors on portable stoves that were set in the floors. The city was divided into various neighborhoods for different sections of the population. There was, for example, a separate section for craftspeople and another section for foreigners.

The Zapotecs

Another great pre-Columbian civilization of the Preclassic and Classic periods was that of the Zapotecs, who originated in the Oaxaca Valley in southern Mexico around 1500 BCE. Around 500 BCE, the Zapotecs built the great urban complex of Monte Albán, which flourished until around 500 CE. The city was built on the leveled-off top of a mountain and consisted of a great plaza surrounded by ceremonial buildings. The inscribed stelae (commemorative pillars), platform temples, and mural **frescoes** in the tombs suggest influences from the Olmecs and the citizens of Teotihuacán. The Zapotecs practiced ancestor worship, and many large burial urns have been found in their tombs.

The Toltecs

The Postclassic period, the final era of pre-Columbian civilization, lasted from around 900 CE until the arrival of colonists from Europe (the end date for the Postclassic period is generally given as 1540 CE). The first people to dominate Central America during this period were the Toltecs, who came to prominence in central and southern Mexico during the tenth and eleventh centuries CE. Their capital, Tula, was 40 miles (64 km) north of modern Mexico City. The stone reliefs carved into the city walls of Tula reflect a social order maintained by force of arms. One pyramid at Tula is partially surrounded by a freestanding wall depicting stone serpents, while on top of the pyramid stand mighty stone warriors, 15 feet (4 m) tall, which held up the temple roof. Nearby is a rack on which the heads of sacrificial human victims were displayed.

It is thought that the Toltecs may have invaded the Yucatán Peninsula around 1000 CE and conquered the Maya city of Chichén Itzá. Many of the buildings at Chichén Itzá appear to be built in the

Toltec style and display Toltec-like carvings. However, it may be that the two cities simply traded with each other and that Toltec styles merely influenced the later architecture of Chichén Itzá.

Tarascans and Mixtecs

Although the Tarascans from western Mexico were prominent from around 1000 BCE until their demise at the hands of the Spaniards in the sixteenth century CE, they achieved their greatest power and influence during the Postclassic period. Their capital was Tzintzuntzan on Lake Pátzcuaro. The Tarascans are noted above all for their circular temples, metalwork, textiles, shields, and feather headdresses.

The Mixtecs took over the Oaxaca Valley in the tenth century CE and built Yagul, together with other cities and ceremonial sites, notably Mitla. The Mixtecs were best known for their mosaic work, which is seen in their masks and on their walls. They were outstanding metalworkers and woodcarvers and are particularly remembered for their cylindrical slit-drums. Mixtec pottery was found throughout Mexico by the fourteenth century CE.

This ritual figurine is a relic of the Chibcha (or Muisca) civilization of the northern Andes.

Andean Civilizations

The Chibcha (also known as the Muisca) were an ancient people who probably inhabited the northern Andes long before the Incas, whom they resembled. Although they built no cities, the Chibcha established a hierarchical culture in which priests governed. The common people were organized into tribes and included craftsmen, traders, farmers, and warriors. The Chibcha practiced irrigation, worked gold, and wove cotton cloth. They kept slaves and made human sacrifices to their chief deities—the sun god and the moon god. Because the chiefs wore golden clothing, it is possible that this region inspired the legend of El Dorado, a fabulous country of unlimited gold.

The **Tiwanaku** civilization arose around 300 BCE in the mountains of present-day Bolivia. It was an important power for several centuries, but little is known about its culture. A temple and several buildings still survive near Lake Titicaca, and archaeologists have established that the Tiwanaku created elaborate textiles and pottery beakers in the likeness of animals. The Tiwanaku—whose culture had vanished by 1200 CE— are the ancestors of the modern Aymara Indians of highland Bolivia.

The Chimú flourished on the Peruvian coast from the ninth century to the fifteenth century CE. Their capital, Chan Chan, covered 6 square miles (15 sq km) and was surrounded by a wall that was 30 feet (9 m) tall. The Chimú developed an extensive system of irrigation to transport water to their farms.

The Coming of the Europeans

All the pre-Columbian cultures that survived into the late fifteenth century CE were brought to an end by the coming of the Spanish. Many of the indigenous peoples who were not slain by the Europeans were wiped out by the diseases that the invaders brought with them and to which the natives had no acquired resistance.

Today, Central America and South America are sometimes referred to as Latin America. This is because Spanish and Portuguese settlers introduced their Latinate romance languages to the region. The Europeans, in turn, were introduced to agricultural products that were—at least originally—only native to the Americas. New World commodities such as wool, tobacco, rubber, chocolate, tomatoes, corn, and potatoes quickly became mainstays on the other side of the Atlantic.

The Temple of the Warriors at the Mayan city of Chichén Itzá is topped with a distinctive chacmool sculpture—a reclining figure resting on its elbows, with its head turned out 90 degrees.

CHAPTER TWO

The Mayan Civilization

The great civilization of the Maya was one of the longest-lasting pre-Columbian cultures, spanning all three of the periods—the Preclassic (ca. 1500 BCE–300 CE), the Classic (ca. 300–900 CE), and the Postclassic (ca. 900–1540 CE). In their heyday, the Maya took Mesoamerican culture to unprecedented heights, scoring great achievements in mathematics, art, and writing. In the ninth century CE, however, the civilization went into rapid decline. Though they held on for several more centuries, the Maya were ultimately conquered by Spanish invaders in the early sixteenth century CE.

The Maya were descended from hunter-gatherers who settled in the Petén region of Guatemala around 300 BCE. That area became the earliest center of Mayan culture. Other hunter-gatherers of the same ancestry settled in El Salvador and Honduras and, by 600 CE, became culturally dominant in those regions. The people who gave the Mayan culture its name began migrating to the Yucatán Peninsula of Mexico in the Classic period; that region then became the center of their civilization.

Mayan Agriculture

During the Preclassic period, the Maya were nomadic and subsisted by hunting, fishing, and gathering. Eventually, they settled in small villages and began to grow corn, using slash-and-burn techniques to clear the jungle for cultivation. Left alone, jungle soil is fertile, with lush green plant life, but when the Maya cut down the forest to make way for cultivated crops, they denuded the land of its nutrients. As a result, the people ran out of food and were often forced to move on and start over in another area. This method of cultivation—which reaped short-term benefits but created insuperable long-term difficulties—forced the Maya to keep moving and thereby determined their lifestyle until the fourth century CE.

By the end of the Preclassic period, Mayan farmers living in swampy areas had learned to build raised plots of land for growing crops and to use the surrounding water channels for irrigation. The Maya of the Classic and Postclassic eras, along with the people of other pre-Columbian civilizations, remained dependent on agriculture. Extended families—large domestic units consisting of parents, children, and grandparents—lived together in small thatched houses. Typically, half of each house was used for cooking and eating, while the other half of the house contained raised platforms used as sleeping quarters. The families worked the land that was held in common by each village, and each community had an administrator (or local chief) who was appointed by the hereditary overall ruler.

The Maya had no draft animals, such as horses, so the farmers had to do a great deal of heavy work. Their main crop was corn, but they also grew beans, squash, and cassava. Cassava, which is also called manioc, is a tropical plant that can grow up to 8 feet (2.4 m) tall, while its fat, potato-like roots can spread to 3 feet (0.9 m) in diameter; manioc roots are the source of tapioca. The sap of the cassava plant can be used to make an alcoholic drink.

The Maya also cultivated cacao trees and used the valuable cacao beans both for food and as a form of currency. Cacao trees can grow to 20 feet (6 m) in height and produce around six thousand blossoms a year, although only around thirty of the blossoms form seedpods. The beans inside the cacao pods—which are almost 12 inches (0.3 m) long—are the size of almonds. Highly nutritious, cacao beans are the original source of chocolate.

The Maya grew cotton, which they turned into textiles by spinning, weaving, and dyeing. Mayan craftsmen made pottery decorated with elaborate scenes from the lives of their rulers or from mythology. Other pottery might be incised, with cinnabar (mercury sulfide, commonly known as red lead) rubbed into the designs. Craftsmen also worked gold, silver, and copper into jewelry and carved pendants, pins, and masks.

Ceremonial Architecture

The Mayan civilization was divided into several small states, each of which was governed by an *ajaw* (hereditary monarch). Most of the states were no larger than a capital city and a small area of land surrounding it, but some of the most powerful states extended their influence over all their smaller neighbors. Each Mayan kingdom had its own ceremonial center, consisting of magnificent pyramids, temples, and palaces built of stone. In view of the fact that the Maya had no metal tools or beasts of burden, those structures were magnificent architectural achievements. Each ceremonial center had a standardized design, consisting of buildings for religious and administrative purposes grouped around a central plaza. The ceremonial centers had no streets and perhaps not even any houses, although it is possible that there were some private residences made of wood that have since disappeared.

The ruins of ceremonial centers have been found in Palenque in the Usumacinta River Basin; in Tikal and Uaxactún in the Petén region; in Uxmal, Mayapán, and Chichén Itzá in the Yucatán Peninsula;

The platform temple at the city of Palenque, which sits atop a stone pyramid, is a typical example of Mayan architecture. The building features a mansard roof—a roof with a two-tiered slope, the lower steeper than the upper.

and in Copán in Honduras. All of these centers have similar site plans and almost identical structures, and some of them are believed to have been cities.

Each center had several platforms topped with temples or palaces and built around the traditional open plaza. The platforms consisted of a core of earth, rubble, or limestone, generally held together with cement, then faced with cut stone and finished off with a plaster facade. The platform temple at Palenque, which was built during the Classic period, is a typical example of Mayan architecture. Some 228 feet (69 m) in length, it stands on a pyramidal platform of cut stones and features a mansard roof (a roof with two slopes on all sides, one steeper than the other) with a cresteria (roof comb) at the top. On higher ground stand three religious buildings that are now known as the Temple of the Cross, the Temple of the Sun, and the Temple of the Foliated Cross. Pictographs describing historical events are inscribed on some of the walls of the temples.

The great buildings were constructed of stones cut to size (with implements made from obsidian) and then rolled into place on wooden poles. They fitted together so well that mortar was not generally required to hold them in place. Some roofs were constructed of corbeled vaults (false arches) by stepping the various layers of stone until they met above the center of the interior.

The walls were massive and usually had no windows, making the inside of the buildings very dark. It is thought to have been the absence of natural light that inspired the Maya to paint the interiors in a range of vivid colors.

The external walls were inlaid with stone mosaics and painted in horizontal patterns in which friezes of decoration alternated with expanses of plain stone. Decorations were carved into the wooden door lintels. The Maya also sculpted large wooden statues and painted them in bright colors.

Residential Cities

In addition to the ceremonial centers, there were several cities in the conventional sense, with streets and residences. Each city had a central square, and the buildings around it served a religious or administrative function. The buildings typically included temples, living quarters for priests, and large palaces with many rooms and pillared galleries. The urban plan included ball courts, elevated causeways, and water reservoirs. Tikal, for example, had so many reservoirs for its population of seventy thousand that water was readily available even during prolonged periods of drought.

Rich people and poor people lived in separate residential districts. Houses for the social elite were built of stone and elaborately decorated and plastered. There is little sign of any kitchens, but it is possible that food was prepared outdoors or in detached wooden structures that have not survived. Many archaeologists and historians believe that the lower classes lived in thatched, wooden structures similar to those used by their modern descendants, but any such period buildings have since disintegrated or been destroyed.

The city square was used as a marketplace. Traders from far-flung places would gather to buy and sell produce; the commercial routes of the Maya covered a vast territory. Tikal, for example, had trading ties with Teotihuacán, some 562 miles (900 km) distant. The merchants either carried their goods on their backs overland or in dugout canoes along rivers. The villages in the lowlands traded textiles, pottery, feathers, cacao, honey, salt, rubber, and wax. The people of the highlands were famous for the production of obsidian (volcanic glass), jade, cotton, gold, and copper.

Major Cities

El Mirador in Petén was probably the largest settlement during the Preclassic period. The city consisted of two groups of pyramids facing each other across a connecting causeway. Its major temple, the Dante Pyramid, is 230 feet (70 m) tall, while another, El Tigre, is 180 feet (55 m) tall.

Chichén Itzá, located on the Yucatán Peninsula, was the most important Mayan city during the Postclassic period. Its name (meaning "Mouth of the wells of Itzá") derived from the fact that it had two natural wells belonging to the Itzá, a prominent Mayan subgroup that inhabited the city. Chichén Itzá was originally built in the early sixth century CE, but it was abandoned in 670 CE—only to be reconstructed

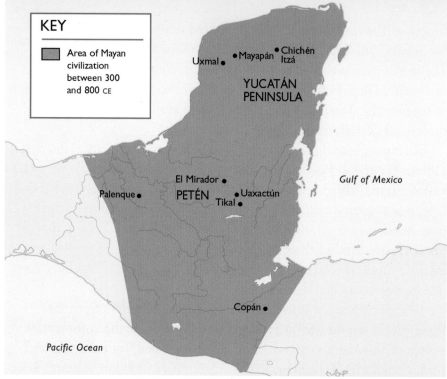

KEY

Area of Mayan civilization between 300 and 800 CE

Uxmal • • Mayapán • Chichén Itzá

YUCATÁN PENINSULA

El Mirador • Palenque • PETÉN • Uaxactún Tikal •

Gulf of Mexico

Copán •

Pacific Ocean

three hundred years later. In 1000 CE, the Toltecs captured Chichén Itzá and made it their own capital, but they, in turn, abandoned the city at least a century before it was captured by Spain in 1531 CE.

Chichén Itzá covers an area of 1 square mile (2.6 sq km). The city's main temple, El Castillo, is dedicated to the god **Quetzalcoatl** and rises 100 feet (30 m) above a pyramid platform that covers an area of 1 acre (4,046 sq m). El Castillo has a staircase on each of its four sides, which is unusual for Mayan structures of this type.

The city has a ball court for the Mayan ritual game of *ulama* (see sidebar, pages 24–25) and a palace named La Casa de las Monjas (The Nunnery). The most notable structure in Chichén Itzá is a stone observatory known as the Caracol (Round Tower), with an unusual circular, snail-shaped staircase inside. It was built by the Toltecs around 1050 CE.

Social Structure

By the end of the Preclassic period, Mayan society had evolved into a series of city-states that were controlled by a strong elite class. The city-states demonstrated their strength and extended their territory through warfare and conquest. By those means, the cities gained access to valuable products from other regions, and the people they conquered were forced to work and fight for them. The Maya did not restrict their aggression to foreign peoples; the Maya of the Yucatán warred among themselves, particularly in the Postclassic period.

The richer and more powerful a city, the more laborers it had at its disposal and the more monuments it could build. It was the elite of the city who controlled the construction and maintenance of its monuments, and most of the stone buildings were regularly maintained and often completely renovated. The work was invariably carried out by the common people.

Mayan society was hierarchical. In the highest echelon were the priests, the military commanders, and the political leaders. These people retained power by making their offices hereditary. A hierarchy of professions was found among the common people as well, with some occupations being placed higher in the social order and accorded greater respect than others. Archaeological discoveries of pottery, wall paintings, and statues have revealed that Mayan creativity was not restricted to handicrafts; it also extended to music and writing.

Mayan Script

No other culture in Mesoamerica developed the art of writing to as high a level as the Maya. Like the ancient Egyptians, the Maya developed a hieroglyphic script consisting of numerous signs and pictures, each of which might represent a whole word, a syllable, or a concept—in each instance, the meaning had to be extrapolated from the context. The Mayan script, which has not yet been fully deciphered, was sophisticated enough to be used to describe details of astronomy, religious worship, and major events in history. It was particularly important in recording dynastic histories, or genealogies.

Mayan scribes generally wrote on paper made from the bark of trees. Sometimes, they wrote on one long strip that they then folded over to make a kind of book known as a **codex**. The four Mayan codices that have survived deal with a wide range of subjects, principally methods of farming and hunting, meteorology, astronomy, and illness.

The Mayan Ball Game

Most Mayan cities had a ball court, and some had more than one. In El Tajin, eleven courts have been found. The courts were used to play the ball game known as ulama, which usually had a religious significance.

Ulama was played on a stone floor flanked by two parallel sloping walls. The walls of the largest court, at Chichén Itzá, were 274 feet (83.5 m) long, 30 feet (12 m) high, and 99 feet (30 m) apart. A small stone ring was set high up on each wall. The game was played between two teams, and the aim was to get the solid rubber ball, around 8 inches (20 centimeters) in diameter, through the rings. The players were not allowed to use their hands or feet to hit the ball, so they had to use their forearms, elbows, and hips.

The players wore protective padding on their hips, knees, shoulders, and arms. Because the ball had to be kept off the ground for as long as possible, the players had to move around rapidly, often sliding to the ground to keep the ball in the air.

It is thought that the game symbolized an episode from the **Popol Vuh** (the *Book of the Community*) in which the mythological twins Hunahpu and Xbalanque battle the underworld. In artistic representations, the twins are shown wearing the ballplayers' shoulder and hip protectors. The players also symbolized other important themes in Mayan religion, including death and rebirth and the cycle of the planets.

Players strove more than usually hard to win because the defeated team was often sacrificed to the gods. The

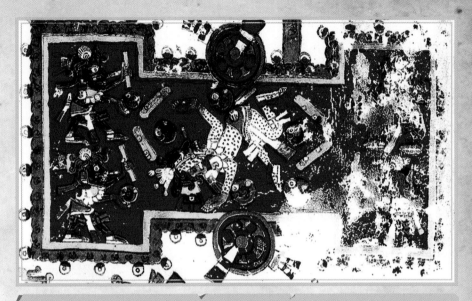

This page from the Codex Borgia, one of the rare surviving Mesoamerican manuscripts, depicts a game of ulama. In the game, players attempted to get a rubber ball through one of two stone rings, shown here as red discs at the top and bottom of the image.

losers might be hurled from a great height or have their heads cut off. Many of the ball courts were surrounded by rows of skulls as a warning and an incentive.

A ruler might also play the game as a means of legitimizing his authority, claiming to be the personification or the descendant of a god. However, if he lost, he did not need to sacrifice himself; he was allowed to pick a prisoner to die in his place.

Because the ball courts had little room for spectators, it is thought that only the elite watched the game. It is also possible that the outcome of matches was determined before they began.

Mayan hieroglyphics, carved in stone, functioned both as writing and as decoration.

The Maya also used hieroglyphs for decorative effect, painting or carving them on their buildings. They inscribed hieroglyphs on numerous surfaces, notably door lintels, stairways, and stelae (monuments). Mayan stelae were generally tall, slender slabs of stone bearing images of the person they honored and a hieroglyphic description of his personal and family history, with particular stress on his great achievements.

Three Calendars

Although the Maya did not invent the calendar, they developed it into the most accurate system of chronology known before the introduction of the Gregorian calendar in 1582 CE. Most of the pre-Columbian cultures used a version of one of the Mayan calendars.

The first Mayan calendar involved a period of 260 days and was possibly based on the human gestation period. It was divided into thirteen cycles that each had twenty days; each day was given a number and a name.

The second calendar was solar (based on the variations in the sun's position in the sky throughout the year). It divided the year into eighteen months that each had twenty days. The five days that remained at the end (to make a total of 365 days) were widely regarded as inauspicious, so people tended to spend them in fasting or in making additional sacrifices. Because the Mayan solar calendar made no allowance for the extra quarter day (as present-day calendars do, with a leap year every four years), it gradually moved out of sequence with the actual timing of the annual seasons.

The two Mayan calendars began on the same day only once every fifty-two years. That fifty-two-year cycle was known as the calendar round. The Maya held no special celebration to mark the end of a cycle. Aztecs, however, traditionally marked the end of a cycle by destroying everything in their individual households in order to start anew. Collectively, the Aztecs also sacrificed a human being; his heart was torn out and a fire was built in his chest to signify cleansing and renewal.

In the third Mayan calendar, known as the Long Count, dates were calculated from the mythological beginning of the world, a date that corresponds to 3114 BCE in Gregorian-based reckoning.

Religion

Mayan religion reflected the culture's dependence on agriculture and the forces of nature, and for that reason, many of the gods were identified with natural phenomena such as wind, rain, and lightning. Itzamna was the god of the sky, and Chac was the god of rain. Other important gods were the sun god, the jaguar god, the corn god, and the moon goddess.

A major part of Mayan religious observance consisted of ceremonies and rituals inspired by the creation myth of *Popol Vuh*, a book that described the supposed origins of the world. The story, which portrays the ancestors of the Mayan elite and their families as gods and demigods, was used by the ruling classes to convince the rest of the Mayan people of their divine right to govern.

Mayan religious practices also included occasional human sacrifices. The Maya believed that the gods needed human blood to strengthen them and that, in return for a sacrifice, the gods would be more willing to look kindly on the endeavors of the Mayan people. The victims were usually prisoners taken in battle, and the traditional method of sacrifice was to cut the heart out of the living victim with a flint knife, after which the body might be hurled down the steps of the pyramid.

Family Life

The clan played a major role in Mayan society. Each clan consisted of a group of interrelated families who lived close together in individual houses. The family was a self-sufficient unit. Most Maya were farmers

Burial Practices

After death, ordinary Mayan people were usually buried in their own homes or in the immediate vicinity. Their bodies were painted red and wrapped in straw matting with a few personal possessions. People of high station received more elaborate funerals than commoners. They were dressed in fine clothes and entombed in a pyramid.

This jade burial mask was found inside the tomb of King Pacal in the Mayan city of Palenque.

If the deceased was rich, he might be buried with some of his slaves, together with jewelry and other items that would be useful in the next world. One tomb, discovered in 1952 CE, contained a sarcophagus of carved stone in which were the remains of King Pacal adorned with gold and jade. The lid of the sarcophagus was inscribed with a scene showing Pacal at the moment of death falling rapturously into the underworld, through the center of which grows the tree of life. The Maya worshipped their ancestors, whom they believed would return to help them in times of need.

who grew their own produce. Work was strictly divided between the sexes. The men were responsible for growing the crops of corn, beans, and cotton, while the women were responsible for growing other vegetables and for looking after the turkeys that most families kept in their yards. The women also made the clothes, cooked the food, and cleaned the house.

Before a marriage could be sanctioned by the Mayan authorities, the man had to pay a dowry to the family of his intended wife. The man would have to work to raise the required amount, and he often took a job with his prospective in-laws. Once the man had earned sufficient money to pay the dowry, the couple married and usually moved into the house of the groom's parents, thereby becoming part of that extended family.

Mayan clothing was relatively simple. The women generally wore shifts (loose-fitting dresses), while the men wore loincloths. When the weather was cold, they would drape themselves in blankets. The men wore their hair in decorative braids and painted or tattooed their bodies. Some Maya also ground down their teeth or inlaid them with gold or jade, a custom that is still practiced in parts of Central America today.

The Civilization in Decline

During the ninth century CE, at the end of the Classic period, the Maya of the Guatemalan lowlands moved away, some to the Guatemalan highlands and others to the Yucatán Peninsula. The reason for the exodus is unclear, but it may have been caused by overpopulation, an unrecorded foreign invasion, or the disruption of trade routes. It is also possible that the Maya were devastated by disease or that the dispersal was forced by climate change or an environmental disaster, such as flooding.

Mayan kings and priests lost power, and Chichén Itzá, the largest surviving city, was ruled by a council of the elite. By the fourteenth century CE, Mayan society had fragmented, and an uneasy alliance of city-states, centered on Mayapán, took over. Mayan civilization ended when the Spanish **conquistadores** gained control of Guatemala in 1525 CE and the Yucatán Peninsula in 1541 CE.

This seventeenth-century CE German engraving is an artist's depiction of the Great Pyramid in the center of Tenochtitlán at the height of Aztec power.

CHAPTER THREE

The Aztec Empire

Although it was comparatively short-lived, the Aztec Empire was a powerful force in the pre-Columbian world. After emerging in the fourteenth century CE, the Aztecs reached their peak in the fifteenth century CE, when they dominated the central and southern parts of present-day Mexico. Their civilization was then quickly wiped out after the arrival of Spanish forces in the sixteenth century CE.

The ancestors of the Aztecs were nomadic hunters who called themselves Mexica. They originally inhabited northern Mexico, but in the twelfth century CE, they started to move southward in search of better living conditions. Their migration ended, after more than a century, at Lake Texcoco, an area that was then under the control of the Tepanecs.

The Tepanecs allowed the Mexica to settle on a couple of small marshy islands in the lake, islands that other peoples had probably rejected as a dwelling place. The early Mexica settlers fed themselves by catching fish in the lake and trapping water birds in nets. However, they still needed land on which to grow crops, and for want of any alternative, they piled up the mud of the lake bed to make chinampas (artificial islands), which they planted with vegetables and corn. Soon, the lake was covered with artificial islands. Canals facilitated boat transportation, causeways were built as links to the mainland, and aqueducts were constructed to bring in fresh water.

For a time, the Mexica had to pay tribute to the Tepanecs in exchange for the land, and they were obliged to serve in the Tepanec army. The Mexica gradually gained a reputation as fierce warriors and eventually became a threat to the Tepanecs themselves.

Around 1345 CE, the Mexica lake dwellings grew into the city of Tenochtitlán, on the site of present-day Mexico City. By 1400 CE, Tenochtitlán had become so powerful that it was able to form a league with the cities of Texcoco and Tlacopán. Together, they declared war on the Tepanecs and conquered the Tepanec cities.

Tenochtitlán was the strongest member of the alliance. With its allies, it soon conquered the other surrounding city-states and became the capital of an extensive realm that was subsequently referred to as the Aztec Empire. As the empire expanded, the Aztecs' new government concentrated almost exclusively on warfare and conquest. The tribes that had once paid tribute to the Tepanecs were now subject to the Aztecs.

Social Structures

The Aztecs were initially divided into two groups: the *pipiltin* (nobles) and the *macehualtin* (common people). Several subdivisions of rank and class determined where people should live and what they should wear. A person's status was fixed at birth and was the same as that of his or her ancestors; there was virtually no social mobility.

The head of the Aztec state was the king, or **tlatoani** (meaning "he who has the word" in Nahuatl, the language of the Aztecs). In addition to the king, who handled **secular** matters, there was an elected male official called the *cihuacoatl* (meaning "woman serpent"), who held the priestly power and dressed in female clothing when conducting religious ceremonies. The tlatoani and the cihuacoatl divided all the power between them.

The king was assisted by members of the nobility, who acted as political advisors, administrators, and priests. A new king was always elected by the nobles from among the most talented members of the royal family. The nobles also constituted the military elite of the state.

The macehualtin were the farmers, craftspeople, and merchants. On the lowest rung of the social ladder were the slaves, most of whom had been captured in war or purchased in the thriving slave markets. Others had sold themselves into slavery in return for food and shelter. Anyone who was unable to pay his debts, who stole, or who committed

This feather headdress may have been worn by Montezuma II, the last Aztec king.

a murder could be enslaved. However, slaves could become free again if they paid off their debts. The children of slaves were born free.

In addition to the class system, Aztec society was divided into administrative units known as calpullis. A calpulli consisted of a group of interrelated families, and each calpulli was assigned a piece of land to be cultivated by all its members. A calpulli might also be responsible for a specialty skill, such as making salt, weaving mats, creating pottery, or brewing pulque (the Aztecs' sacred drink, made from the fermented juice of the maguey, a species of cactus). Each calpulli also had its own temple and school. Those institutions gave instruction in religion and handicrafts, and trained the young men as warriors. In times of war, the calpulli supplied troops to the king. In peacetime, the workmen of the calpulli served the public agencies in the city.

Provincial Divisions

The Aztec Empire was divided into around thirty-five provinces. When a tribe was vanquished by the Aztecs, the original leaders were frequently allowed to retain their positions on condition that they served the Aztecs. The leaders were even accepted into the Aztec nobility, and their children were educated in Tenochtitlán so that they could, in due course, take over their fathers' positions.

The provinces had to pay annual tributes to the king, and each province had an official who was responsible for ensuring that the tribute was actually paid. The nature of the tribute was determined by the distance of the province from Tenochtitlán. Provinces that were near to the capital were usually required to pay their tributes in corn. Outlying provinces had to pay tribute in the form of feathers, which were lighter and therefore easier to transport.

The Merchant Class

The *pochtecas* (merchants) formed a separate class. They commanded greater respect than farmers and craftspeople, but they were equally obliged to pay tribute to the king. Some merchants, unlike other members of the macehualtin, were allowed to own land, and their sons were educated at the schools of the elite.

The merchants imported essential goods from outside the city, but that was not their only function. Because they traveled throughout the entire Aztec territory and frequently went beyond its borders to trade, they were well placed to act as spies and feed the intelligence they gathered back to Tenochtitlán. Their ability to speak foreign languages and adapt to the ways of foreign peoples made it easy for them to engage in espionage in hostile countries.

Warfare

The Aztec state did not maintain a large standing (permanent) army, but all Aztec men were expected to fight when the king went to war. Military training for young men began at the age of fifteen. Every new recruit wore a tuft of hair at the back of his head until he had taken a captive, after which the tuft could be removed. After a youth had taken four captives, he was acknowledged as a fully fledged warrior.

The Aztecs had no iron, so they used weapons that were made mainly of wood, although they were able to make sharp blades from

Aztec Writing

The Aztecs developed a form of pictographic script (writing based on small pictures). Some of their pictures represented ideas, while others stood for syllables of words. Like the Maya, the Aztecs used a form of paper made from tree bark, long strips of which were folded to form books called codices.

The Aztecs' pictographic writing was used mainly to keep records of tax receipts, business transactions, and censuses. Only scribes could read and write, and most of the scribes were priests.

From the pictographic books that have survived, much can be gleaned about the daily life of the Aztecs. One codex includes depictions of a band of musicians, a law court, a troupe of acrobats, and prisoners in jail. Some books show the Aztecs' ritual calendar, depicting each day with its associated god, while other manuscripts include portraits of the gods and scenes of human sacrifice.

obsidian (volcanic glass). The warriors wore feathered headdresses and quilted cotton suits, and they carried leather-covered shields. Rather than engage in hand-to-hand combat, they often fought at a distance, using bows, slings, and blowpipes. One of the most important objectives of Aztec warfare was to take as many live captives as possible back to Tenochtitlán, where they were sacrificed to the gods. Sometimes, conflicts known as **flower wars** were waged, with the specific object not of obtaining tribute but of capturing people.

Gods and Sacrifices

The religion of the Aztecs was extremely complex. There were a great many gods, all of whom could change their nature, a concept known

This calendar stone, unearthed in present-day Mexico City, outlines the Aztec worldview.

as dualism. The central figure, however, was the sun god, Tonatiuh. The Aztecs believed that four previous worlds (each with its own sun and sun god) had existed and been destroyed. The Aztecs also believed that the fifth world—their world—had been created in the fire of the ruins of Teotihuacán. Aztec priests and astrologers predicted that the fifth world would be destroyed by earthquakes.

A "calendar stone" (found under the central square of Mexico City where the Great Pyramid of Tenochtitlán once stood) records some Aztec cosmological beliefs. The stone combines the shape of Tonatiuh with an image of the earth monster, Tlaltecuhtli (who had clawed hands and a knife tongue). Around this dual image are symbols of the four previous worlds and their destruction.

The twin temples that stood on top of the Great Pyramid of Tenochtitlán were dedicated to two gods (the rain god, Tlaloc, and the war god, Huitzilopochtli) and reflected the importance of agriculture and war in Aztec society. The god Tezcatlipoca (Smoking Mirror) had a special function. He was associated with death, night, magic, justice, and battle, but he was simultaneously an aspect of the other gods. The

Aztecs believed that Tezcatlipoca knew what they were thinking and, indeed, the secrets of the whole world.

The Aztecs further believed that the gods had to receive regular offerings of human blood in order to remain strong. Hence, human sacrifice was a regular part of Aztec worship. Such offerings were made to please the gods and to secure their assistance in warding off evil and ensuring good harvests and success in battle. The manner in which the sacrificial victims were killed varied according to the purpose of the offering, the god for whom the sacrifice was intended, and the time of year when it was carried out.

The Aztecs used two calendars, both of which had been in existence for centuries and had previously been employed by the Maya. The first calendar divided the year into eighteen months that each had twenty days. The five days that were added to make a total of 365 days for each year were considered a time of danger. The second calendar included 260 days divided into thirteen periods that each had twenty days. This second calendar was a ritual calendar that specified the days on which religious festivals and sacrifices were to take place.

This illustration from the sixteenth-century CE *Codex Magliabechiano* shows an Aztec ritual sacrifice.

Every twenty days, a religious festival was held to celebrate the change of period. The celebrations featured songs, dances, processions, and often human sacrifices. The victims were usually prisoners of war or, occasionally, slaves. The victims were first ritually washed, and then they were dressed in beautiful clothes and painted in the style of the god to whom they were about to be offered. The victims were lined up on the steps of the temple and then, one by one, laid on the sacrificial stone. Their chests were slashed open with knives made of obsidian, and their hearts were torn out and placed in a bowl. Their bodies were

The Capital City

Tenochtitlán, the city built on the site of modern Mexico City, was the center of the Aztec Empire. The city was built on a lake, and there were three causeways connecting it with the shore. When the Spanish conquistadores came upon the city for the first time at the beginning of the sixteenth century CE, they were amazed. It was larger than any city in Europe at that time, and it had a population of around 250,000. It consisted of enormous stone pyramids and temples, together with administrative buildings and houses, interspersed with roads and a network of canals, along which the inhabitants traveled by boat. Aqueducts brought fresh water into the city, and there was a sophisticated sewer system.

At the center of the city was the Great Pyramid, part of a complex that included ceremonial monuments, plazas, and stone stairways; the whole area was surrounded by a stone wall. A double staircase led from the ground to the top of the Great Pyramid, and on top of the pyramid stood the twin temples dedicated to Huitzilopochtli (the war god) and Tlaloc (the rain god). Part of the temple shrine was the stone on which sacrificial victims were laid before their hearts were cut out.

Outside the stone wall were the houses of the nobility. These large, flat-roofed, two-story houses were built of stone or mud bricks and had living rooms, bedrooms, kitchens, and separate rooms for servants—all arranged around a patio. A few houses had steam baths. The nobles were the only people allowed to have two-story houses. The rest of the city was divided into ten-house and hundred-house units. These houses, for the common people, were much simpler. Groups of citizens of the same profession or same status lived in the same district.

then hurled down the temple steps. Sometimes, the sacrificial victims were beheaded, and at other times, the victims were burned alive, shot with arrows, or hurled to their deaths from a great height. The skulls of the victims were displayed on a rack near the Great Pyramid.

Everyday Life

Most Aztecs lived in simple houses that were usually built from stone with roofs made of branches. The homes often had no windows. Poorer people generally lived in oval huts made of stakes and roofed with reeds.

Inside the houses, round earthenware pots were used to store provisions. The beds were simple reed mats, and sometimes, there was a wooden chest for personal objects. The houses also contained the occupants' work tools and earthenware pots and pans for cooking. There was frequently a mortar for grinding corn. At night, Aztec homes were illuminated by flaming torches.

Children and adolescents went to school, where they were taught good behavior and given instruction in combat, handicrafts, and religion. The Aztecs had extremely strict rules of conduct. Young people were taught how to interact with their elders, the correct way of walking through the streets, and the right clothes to wear on every occasion. There were rules about the chores children might do at any specific age and about the amount of food that they were allowed to eat. Outside school, it was the general practice that boys were brought up by their fathers and girls were brought up by their mothers. Girls were mainly concerned with household tasks and preparing themselves for marriage.

Clothing was designed to reflect the status of the wearer. Only members of the nobility were allowed to wear cotton, and their clothes were often expensive and brightly colored. In particular, the ceremonial robes of the nobles were richly decorated.

The priests wore clothing and ornaments designed to reflect the appearance of the gods they served. They put pins and rings in their ears, lips, and noses, and wore sumptuous gold and silver jewelry.

The common people dressed simply in cloth made of maguey fiber. The men wore loincloths, while the women wore skirts that reached to their ankles and, sometimes, a rectangular piece of cloth knotted at the right shoulder.

The distinction between the nobles and the common people was reflected in food as well as in clothing. The nobility ate the meat of turkeys and dogs, together with chocolate and fish from the coast. The common people lived mainly on corn, beans, and peppers. The corn was usually consumed in the form of tortillas (thin pancakes made of corn flour and baked on top of heated clay ovens). The most popular beverage was the sacred drink, pulque.

In addition to the food they grew themselves, the people of Tenochtitlán also harvested food from their watery surroundings. Their diet included frogs, worms, and water bugs.

Farming

The principal crop of the Aztecs was corn, but they also grew peppers, pumpkins, and beans. Their farming techniques remained unchanged for centuries. They had no draft animals, so they used simple, long-handled hoes to till the ground.

As the city of Tenochtitlán expanded, the Aztecs brought barren land into cultivation by means of irrigation. In the marshy area around the city, they also created areas of fertile land by building raised island plots. They planted trees around the plots to prevent the earth from being washed away.

Artisans

The artisans in Tenochtitlán lived in separate districts according to their crafts. Potters made pots and cookware, tailors made clothing, and carpenters made the simple furniture used in homes. Headdresses for the warriors were made by feather makers from the quantities of feathers that were sent to the capital as tribute. Sculptors produced statues that were erected throughout the city and in the temples. Many objects were made from obsidian and greenstone (nephrite), while masks and sculptures were made from wood and then covered in elaborate mosaics of turquoise.

The most significant Aztec architectural structure was the pyramid. Pyramids were built of huge stones that were piled on top of each other in layers. Because the Aztecs had no wheels, they rolled the stones to the construction sites on tree trunks laid along the ground. Aztec civil engineering methods required vast numbers of workers.

Territorial Expansion

After the Mexica overcame their rivals, the Tepanecs, in 1428 CE, they began to expand their empire. Tribes that had paid tribute to the Tepanecs became subject to the Mexica, who oriented their new government entirely toward warfare and became the Aztecs.

Around 1458 CE, the Aztecs embarked on a more extensive campaign of expansion under the leadership of Montezuma I (ruled 1440–1468 CE). His conquests were primarily of the Mixtec territories in the southeast. The subjugated Mixtec cities were forced to pay punishing tributes, and many of their citizens were massacred.

Although the initial motivation for conquest had been the desire for territorial expansion, a religious motivation gradually took over. The Aztec gods required an ever-increasing number of human sacrifices, so the need for victims grew accordingly. Thousands of captured enemies were taken back to Tenochtitlán as human sacrifices to satisfy the gods.

Montezuma I was succeeded first by Axayacatl (ruled 1468–1481 CE) and then by Tizoc (ruled 1481–1486 CE). The next king, Ahuitzotl (ruled 1486–1502 CE), conquered large areas of the northern coast in 1487 CE, taking many prisoners for the gods. Ahuitzotl then celebrated the enlargement of the temple dedicated to Huitzilopochtli with a great religious ceremony at which some four thousand people were sacrificed.

Ahuitzotl's successor was **Montezuma II**, the last Aztec king. He died, probably in battle, in 1520 CE. Less than a year later, the Aztec Empire fell to Spanish conquistadores under the leadership of **Hernán Cortés** (1485–1547 CE).

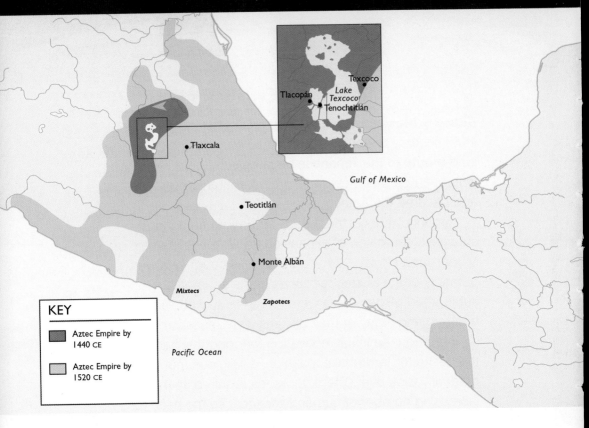

KEY

■ Aztec Empire by 1440 CE

□ Aztec Empire by 1520 CE

The Fall of the Empire

At the beginning of the sixteenth century CE, the Spanish conquistadores destroyed the mighty Aztec Empire with breathtaking rapidity. It took the invaders from Europe just two years (1519–1521 CE) to crush the power of one of the world's great civilizations, which had been two centuries in the making.

The Spanish began their voyage to Central America from Cuba on February 10, 1519 CE. Eleven ships, carrying a total of 508 men, set sail under the leadership of Hernán Cortés. Some historians have reported that, even before the invaders landed, the Aztec emperor Montezuma II (ruled 1502–1520 CE) had been troubled by omens of disaster. Comets had been seen in the sky, and a farmer claimed to have seen mountains moving through the sea—his sightings may have been the ships of Cortés. More important, when Montezuma's spies reported that people with white faces had landed on the coast, the emperor failed to take immediate action because he believed that the invaders were agents of the god-king Quetzalcoatl. According to Aztec legend, Quetzalcoatl

This painted screen from seventeenth-century CE Mexico depicts the fighting between the Aztecs and the conquistadores.

was destined to return that year to seek revenge for having been driven out of the country hundreds of years previously. Montezuma's prediction of the Aztecs' demise turned out to be a self-fulfilling prophecy.

The Spaniards pitched camp on the coast and remained there for several months. During that time, Cortés and Montezuma exchanged messages and gifts. Montezuma's scouts also provided him with detailed information about the newcomers, who, with their pale complexions, beards, and horses, were quite unlike any beings that the Aztecs had ever previously encountered.

Many of the peoples conquered by the Aztecs hated their overlords and joined forces with Cortés as his forces advanced overland toward Tenochtitlán. When the Aztecs finally and belatedly recognized the seriousness of the Spanish threat, the two sides confronted each other. The Aztecs were overwhelmed and surrendered on August 13, 1521 CE. Shortly afterward, many Aztecs died of smallpox, a disease carried by the Spanish and to which the native peoples had no immunity. The Aztecs who avoided or survived the epidemic were then enslaved by their Spanish conquerors.

The Spanish conquistadores completely destroyed the Aztec culture. They demolished the pyramids and temples, and built Christian churches on the ruins. They destroyed the books that contained Aztec picture writing and stole the golden Aztec jewelry, which was melted down and shipped as ingots to Spain.

Some Aztec relics and ruins have survived, however. Today, they silently commemorate a once extraordinary culture. Modern archeological work has uncovered parts of the Great Pyramid of Tenochtitlán, buried under present-day Mexico City. Meanwhile, Nahuatl, the language of the Aztecs, is still spoken to this day.

The Incan city of Machu Picchu was built in the Andes Mountains at an elevation of 7,710 feet (2,350 m). It remained unknown to the outside world until the early twentieth century CE.

CHAPTER FOUR

The Inca Empire

A t its apex, the Inca Empire controlled more land than any other pre-Columbian civilization of South America. Its territory spanned 2,500 miles (4,000 km) along the Pacific coast, from present-day Ecuador in the north to central Chile in the south, and extended 500 miles (800 km) inland. The empire had a population of roughly twelve million people by the fifteenth century CE. The Incas were a dominant force in the region, but their power was fleeting. Like the other great pre-Columbian civilizations of the Americas, the Inca Empire rapidly fell to the Spanish in the sixteenth century.

The region ruled by the Incas encompassed many different types of terrain (mountains, plains, jungles, forests, and deserts), and the people they ruled came from many tribes, spoke many languages, and had numerous different cultures. Nevertheless, the Incas welded this vast territory into one large empire with its own impressive culture.

The Incas were skilled in astronomy, metallurgy, textile design, art, architecture, and farming methods. They built great cities from stone, and the far-flung outposts of their empire were connected by an extensive road network.

The Birth of the Empire

Because the Incas had no writing system, much of their history depends on oral tradition. One Inca origin myth tells of four brothers and four sisters who left a cave and traveled to the Andes region. Three of the brothers died en route, but the fourth brother, Manco Capac, married one of his sisters and settled in the area around Cuzco (the modern city of Cusco, Peru), which became the capital of the Inca Empire.

Parts of that myth are corroborated by anthropological evidence. Members of the Quechua people (the first Incas) migrated around 1100 CE to the Cuzco Valley, where they drove out the existing inhabitants and settled themselves. The newcomers spoke Quechua, which became the language of the Incas and is still spoken today by millions of people in Ecuador, Peru, Bolivia, Chile, and Argentina— all regions that the Inca Empire controlled at its peak.

Until the reign of their eighth king, Viracocha, the Incas did not pursue an aggressive expansionist policy but were content to attack their nearest enemies and take their lands or exact tribute from them. However, when Viracocha came to power around 1435 CE, he conquered an area of some 25 miles (40 km) around Cuzco, setting up permanent rule over the newly conquered lands.

In 1438 CE, Viracocha's kingdom was invaded by the Chancas, an aggressive people who had already conquered an area immediately to the west of the Inca kingdom. By then, Viracocha had already nominated one of his sons, Urqon, to be his successor, but another son, Cusi Yupanqui, had set his own sights on the throne. Civil war threatened, and Viracocha fled, together with Urqon, leaving Cusi Yupanqui in command of the army.

Years of Conquest

Cusi Yupanqui was a great general. He not only routed the invaders but also managed to take new territory while in pursuit of the Chancas. On his triumphant return to the capital, he proclaimed himself king, taking the name Pachacuti Inca Yupanqui.

Pachacuti Inca Yupanqui's brother Capac Yupanqui assisted in the campaign against the Chancas, but when he made the fatal mistake of showing an interest in the throne, he was assassinated. Pachacuti Inca Yupanqui then appointed his own son, Topa Inca Yupanqui, as commander-in-chief.

Topa Inca Yupanqui led his troops north to attack the empire of the Chimu. The Chimu were a desert people who had made their barren lands fertile by irrigation. Now, fearful that the Incas would cut off their vital water supplies, they surrendered and became part of the Inca Empire. Subsequently, as king, Topa Inca Yupanqui campaigned south to the tropical region at the foot of the Andes, where he made further conquests.

In 1493 CE, Topa Inca Yupanqui was succeeded by his son, **Huayna Capac**, who continued to expand the empire into the southern Andes and the region that is now modern Ecuador.

Administrative Divisions

The Inca Empire—known as the Tahuantinsuyu (Empire of the Four Winds)—was divided into four quarters—Cuntisuyu, Chinchasuyu, Antisuyu, and Kollasuyu. The capital of all four regions was Cuzco.

The quarters were subdivided into provinces and smaller administrative and economic areas. The smallest was the extended family landholding unit known as the **ayllu**. The ayllu had both social and administrative functions. Although the land belonging to each ayllu was worked by its family members, its cultivation was supervised by the government, which advised on crops, irrigation and drainage (including large-scale projects), fertilizing, and terracing of the farmland.

Each new king founded his own royal ayllu, which included his noblemen and a great number of ordinary citizens who were obliged to work for the king and the noblemen. A royal ayllu was considered permanent, and it continued to exist even after the king's death.

The Incas believed that when a king died, his reign continued within his ayllu and all the property and wealth within the ayllu remained in his possession. The new leader had to conquer new territory and acquire new wealth in order to be able to found his own ayllu. So, for each new leader, the acquisition of wealth was extremely important. It was not only desirable in itself, but it also enabled the king to lavish gifts on his noblemen to bind them to him.

Conflicts of Succession

Inca society was rigidly organized. At the top was the king, who was not only all-powerful on earth but also retained that power after death.

KEY

Extent of Inca
Empire by
1525 CE

After the royal family, which was thought to be semi-divine, came the aristocracy, the government administrators, the petty nobility, and then the commoners.

One of the recurring problems in Inca society was the battle that generally ensued whenever it was time for a new king. The leadership of the royal Incas was hereditary, but the succession was not always clear-cut. Although the leader would hand over power to a son of his own choosing, there were often other claimants to the throne. The difficulty arose from the fact that Inca men were allowed more than one wife. The king's first wife was usually his full sister, following the precedent set by the founding ruler, Manco Capac. The king would also have a number of secondary wives, who were usually selected from the elite families of the lands he had conquered. All the sons of these wives would have a claim to the throne. Consequently, civil war was almost inevitable when a reigning king died.

Ancestor Worship

Ancestor worship was central to the Inca belief system. The living conducted their affairs in ways that they thought would be approved of by the dead. They were particularly influenced by the supposed wishes of dead kings, whose importance was reflected in royal funeral rites. When a king died, his body was mummified and he continued to "live" in his own home, surrounded by relatives. His possessions were transferred to the *paqana*, a group comprising all of his male descendants (apart from his chosen successor); these descendants controlled his land and ensured that he lacked nothing. The ayllu founded by the living king continued to work his land after his death.

The dead king continued to be deferred to as if he were still alive, and his advice was sought by the living. He was regularly dressed in new clothes, received visitors, was offered food, and was carried on a mat through the city on ceremonial days.

Public Service

Incas were not taxed in the conventional way, by paying money or handing over portions of their produce. Instead, they provided labor to the state and their own ayllus. Every healthy adult male head of a household had to work a specified number of hours every year for both the empire and his family's landholding unit.

Some men cultivated the state's lands; some worked on the construction of public buildings, bridges, and roads; and some served in the army. While an Inca subject was fulfilling his duty to the state, the government paid his board. The income from obligatory labor was used to defray the cost of the distribution of surplus food to the provinces.

The Incas kept numerical records by employing a system of colored and knotted cords known as **quipus**. The accountants and overseers of the imperial administration were known as *quipucamayoc*.

A City in the Mountains

The Inca city of Machu Picchu was never found by the Spaniards. It remained undiscovered by any European until 1911 CE, when the American explorer and archaeologist Hiram Bingham came across it while searching for another lost Inca city, Vilcabamba. A local farmer told him that there were ruins in the mountains, and when Bingham and his party scrambled up a steep incline, they found stone walls and buildings covered in thick vegetation.

The city that Bingham discovered was 50 miles (80 km) northwest of Cuzco and lay on a plateau between two mountain peaks that rose 1,950 feet (600 m) above the Urubamba River. Building a city in this mountainous spot was an engineering feat of considerable magnitude. The houses were built on terraces on the steep hillsides, and the different levels were connected by stone stairways. Below the houses were agricultural terraces on which the inhabitants grew their own food. At the center, on the plateau, was an open plaza where public meetings were held.

The city had two small temples and a stone altar known as an **Intiwatana** (hitching post of the sun). Intiwatanas had special significance for the Incas. At the spring and autumn equinoxes, the sun stands directly above the altar, casting no shadow, and at those times, the Inca priests would symbolically "tie" the sun to the altar to ensure that it would continue to shine on them and bring warmth to Earth. The Spanish knew that Intiwatanas were sacred to the Incas, so they systematically destroyed every one they found; the Intiwatana at Machu Picchu is one of the few that have survived.

The stone altar at Machu Picchu is one of the few remaining examples of an *Intiwatana*, or a hitching post of the sun.

Bingham named the city after one of the two mountains that guard it; the other peak is called Huayna Picchu. "Machu Picchu" means "Old Peak" in the Quechua language, and it is possible that the site was a sacred place from the earliest times. Some archaeologists have surmised that Machu Picchu was not an ordinary city but a special sanctuary, where secret ceremonies were held. Whatever the truth, the city was abandoned by the Incas around 1570 CE and remained hidden and forgotten for the next three and a half centuries.

Religion

The Inca worshipped numerous gods, whose characters and roles might change or overlap. Together, the gods were seen as a spiritual force that ruled the material world. Viracocha (the creator), Inti (the sun god), and Illapa (the god of thunder and the weather) dominated a pantheon that was strongly linked to the forces of nature. Other gods included those of the moon, the stars, the earth, and the sea. The Incas also believed that their kings were descendants of Inti, who protected the empire.

Many of the Incas' religious ceremonies were linked to the planting and harvesting of crops and to medicine. Legends and music played a major part in Inca rituals, at some of which live animals such as llamas and guinea pigs were sacrificed. The Incas also sacrificed children to the gods. Boys and girls, known as *capacochas*, were specially selected from all over the empire and taken to Cuzco at the age of ten. After arriving in the capital, they were given a great feast, dressed in fine clothes, and taken to the imperial altars, where they were sacrificed. After their death, the capacochas were worshipped.

The Incas also venerated **huacas** (local shrines) and visited them regularly to consult at the altars. Almost anything could be a huaca; it might be a sacred place, a sacred object, or the mummified remains of a sacred person.

The Incas imposed their religion and gods on all the peoples they conquered, and each provincial capital followed the example of Cuzco in erecting city altars. However, the Incas were always willing to accommodate the religious practices of the conquered peoples as long as they did not attempt to resist subjugation.

Assimilation and Dissent

The Incas conquered vast territories in rapid succession and resorted to a variety of methods to maintain control of their acquisitions. Local chiefs who surrendered were allowed to remain in office and administer the region on the Incas' behalf. They were obliged to spend four months of every year in Cuzco in order to learn Inca ways. To ensure loyalty, their sons were taken to Cuzco, where they were educated and held hostage.

Any subject chief who rebelled was executed and replaced by a governor. Where whole peoples were troublesome, the Inca government operated a draconian resettlement policy. The rebels were forcibly moved to distant parts of the empire and replaced by people who were loyal to the regime.

Social Classes

Everyone in Inca society had a fixed place and function, which reflected his or her status. One of the most elite groups was the *yanacona*, which consisted of men in the service of the king or a nobleman. The yanaconas were protected by their employer and thus released from the obligations of the common citizens. The yanaconas were chosen from among the sons of the highest classes throughout the provinces and trained to be personal assistants to the king or a nobleman, either living or dead. The office of the yanaconas was hereditary.

The *camayo*—another group of high social rank—consisted of craftsmen, farmers, soldiers, and merchants who were employed full-time in the king's service. Camayos were exempt from taxes and were not required to do military service. Because the camayos were not obliged to reside at court, entire villages might be composed of them. The king granted land to the camayos and provided them with clothing.

The most beautiful daughters of the elite might be selected to serve the king or the sun god from the age of eight or nine. Known as *acllas* (chosen women), they were removed from their homes to be brought up far away from their parents. The acllas lived in closed convents, where they were educated in religious matters. They were taught how to weave ceremonial garments for the priests and how to prepare special foods and the sacred drink, chicha, for religious ceremonies. At the age of sixteen, the acllas were divided into various groups according to their beauty. Some were chosen for sacrifice and considered themselves fortunate because they were assured of happiness in the other world. Others were chosen to live in convents. A third group was taken to Cuzco to serve as royal concubines or to be married off to men the king wanted to favor.

Clothes and Jewelry

The clothes worn by Incas depended on and reflected their social status. Conventional male attire consisted of a loincloth and a

Chimpo Ocllo Coya

This sixteenth-century CE Spanish drawing shows a woman in characteristic Incan attire, including a long tunic and a draped mantle.

sleeveless tunic under a cloak. Men also wore headbands and waistbands around their tunics; the style of both items was prescribed by law according to the individual's position in society. The common people wore clothes made from coarse wool and fibers, while the nobles dressed in cotton and alpaca wool and had intricate designs woven around the necks of their tunics. Most men carried a small, decorated, square bag to hold possessions such as small tools.

Women wore long tunics wound around the body and fastened at the shoulder by a pin. They also wore sashes that indicated their station in life. Over the long tunics, they wore mantles fastened at the front with a *tupu* (a large pin). Noblewomen's jewelry was made of gold or silver, while peasant women wore pins made of wood or copper. Women also wore folded squares of cloth on their heads.

Cloth had an important role in Inca society. Besides distinguishing the status of its wearer, it was also used as a medium of exchange because it was easily carried and traded over long distances. Some communities paid their taxes in cloth, while soldiers and others who performed community service were sometimes paid in cloth.

Clothing also played a key role in ceremonial life. The priests wore special robes, which were highly decorated. When a boy completed his puberty rites, he was given a new set of clothes and new clothes were also given to couples as wedding presents.

Architecture

In spite of having only limited technology at their disposal, the Incas constructed an enormous number of magnificent palaces, temples, houses, roads, and bridges, many of which can still be seen today. For the buildings, the Incas used large blocks of stone, some up to 10 feet (3 m) tall, which they cut and carved into shape so that they fitted together perfectly and did not require mortar.

The huge stone blocks were moved by large crews of construction workers who hauled them into position using wooden rollers on top of graduated earthen ramps. The capital city, Cuzco, contained the royal palace, the administrative buildings, and the Incas' largest temple, the Temple of the Sun. Many of these structures glittered with gold and silver, and the walls of the Temple of the Sun were covered with gold plate so that they shone in sunlight. In the courtyard of the temple, a tableau was created entirely in gold; golden corn appeared to grow in golden earth, while herds of golden llamas grazed on golden grass.

The houses of the ordinary people usually consisted of a single room and were built of mud bricks or stone with a thatched roof. The doorways were tapered, being wider at the bottom than at the top, and many houses had no windows. Extended families lived in groups of as many as eight houses built around a central courtyard that generally had only one entrance. The women did their cooking in these courtyards. The houses were sparsely furnished because the Incas had few personal possessions.

Roads and Bridges

A vast network of roads connected all parts of the empire and converged on Cuzco. The roads served as trading routes to the outlying provinces and allowed runners to facilitate an efficient system of communication to the most distant Inca territories.

When the roads came to rivers and ravines, the Incas built bridges of various types, including rope suspension bridges, one of which was 328 feet (100 m) long. Guards were stationed at strategic points on the roads to protect travelers, repair bridges, and prevent the unauthorized movement of goods.

A Messenger Service

The **chaski** were relay runners who conveyed oral communications throughout the Inca Empire. Runners were stationed at regular intervals along the imperial highway system, and at each stage, the messages were passed from one runner to the next. In that way, a message could travel the 400 miles (650 km) from Cuzco to Lima in as little as three days, while a rider on horseback would take twelve days to complete the same journey. The chaski system extended all over South America, into parts of modern Argentina, Bolivia, Chile, and Colombia.

In order that no time should be wasted on the handovers, chaski runners sounded warning blasts on *pututus* (conch shells) as they neared the next *tambo* (staging post), allowing the next runner to be ready to take up the message and head off without delay. The system was extraordinarily efficient and was only possible because of the remarkable road system that linked all parts of the Inca Empire.

The Fall of the Inca

The Inca Empire reached its greatest extent in the early sixteenth century CE. Its decline began in 1525 CE, when Huayna Capac abandoned a military expedition in northern Ecuador after hearing that Cuzco was gripped by a virulent disease (probably smallpox or measles) that was causing a huge number of deaths. He returned to the capital but was himself immediately struck down and died without naming an heir.

A struggle for power broke out between Huayna Capac's sons, Huascar and Atahuallpa. The ensuing civil war fatally weakened the empire at the very moment when it was confronted with the Spanish, who, under the leadership of **Francisco Pizarro** (ca. 1471–1541 CE), invaded the region from the north.

In 1532 CE, Atahuallpa captured Huascar and began negotiating with the Spaniards, but they took him prisoner in November of that year. While in prison, Atahuallpa arranged for Huascar to be assassinated by drowning. He then offered the Spaniards a roomful of gold in return for his freedom. Pizarro agreed, but after receiving the ransom, he had Atahuallpa strangled.

ATHABALIPA
ultimus Rex Peruanorum

Atahualpa, seen here in a nineteenth-century CE engraving, was imprisoned by the conquistadors in 1532 CE and executed the following year. The Inca Empire fell soon after.

Pizarro then installed Huascar's brother, Manco Capac, on the throne as a puppet king under the Spanish. Manco Capac tried to rebel, but he was forced to flee to the mountains, where he was killed. Tupac Amaru, his youngest son, claimed the Inca throne, but the Spaniards put him to death as well. The ruling dynasty of the Incas thus came to a swift end, and with them, the empire.

This illustration from the late sixteenth century CE depicts a typical Algonquian village of the northeastern United States. The village is palisaded, meaning it is surrounded by a fence of wooden stakes.

CHAPTER FIVE

Native North American Cultures

Centuries before Europeans began to colonize North America, there were already millions of Native Americans residing on the continent. These ancestors of today's Native Americans were divided among a number of different tribes. Though the tribes developed independently of each other, many of them share similar cultural attributes.

No one knows for sure how or when the continent's original inhabitants first reached America, but it seems likely that they came from Asia during the last ice age. At that time, ice and glaciers had trapped so much of the world's water that the level of the oceans was much lower than it is today, and what is now the Bering Strait between Russian Siberia and Alaska was dry land. Around twenty to thirty thousand years ago, the ancestors of the Native Americans probably crossed that land bridge into North America in search of better hunting grounds. During the following centuries, more people crossed from Siberia and dispersed throughout the Americas.

Diverse Tribes

As the newcomers spread throughout the Americas, their languages, customs, and lifestyles began to diverge. The first Native Americans split into hundreds of different groups, and by the time Christopher

Columbus arrived in 1492 CE, there were more than five million people in North America alone. These people were divided among hundreds of tribes and spoke more than two hundred different languages.

Because of the wide variety of native cultures in North America, it is impossible to describe any one way of life as being typical of the entire continent. However, many cultures did share some common characteristics. For example, most native cultures were restricted to a single, small locality. At the end of the fifteenth century CE, no North American societies were as large or as complex as those of the Mayan, Aztec, and Inca empires of Central America and South America. Those empires each had a central government, large cities, an educated elite, and a dynamic economy. In contrast, the societies of North America tended to be simpler, rural, and based on villages.

The Anasazi

In earlier times, North America had seen great urban centers similar to those of the Aztecs, but those civilizations had vanished by the time the Europeans arrived. Around 1000 CE, in southwestern North America, the Anasazi people built large housing complexes, later known as **pueblos**, out of stone and adobe (bricks made of sunbaked mud and straw). One of the largest of those complexes was Pueblo Bonito in modern New Mexico. Many different families lived in each pueblo and farmed the surrounding land.

The region was arid, but the Anasazi were skillful farmers. They dug miles of irrigation canals to water the land, and that allowed them to grow corn, beans, and other vegetables. With ample food, it was not necessary for every Anasazi to work on the land, and this freed up some people to develop an elaborate religious system. Other people became expert weavers, jewelers, or potters. Anasazi potters made artifacts in many shapes and sizes and decorated them with black-and-white geometric designs.

Around 1300 CE, the Anasazi abandoned their pueblos and disappeared. The reasons for that are unknown. It may be that they were attacked and destroyed by a hostile tribe. Alternatively, there may have been a drought that resulted in a famine, or perhaps they had exhausted the supply of wood that was needed for fuel.

Pueblo Bonito

The great housing complex of Pueblo Bonito was built by the Anasazi in Chaco Canyon, New Mexico, between 900 and 1200 CE. It was constructed in a D shape, with the straight edge against the wall of the canyon. Its three stories contained around eight hundred interconnecting rooms and forty underground rooms, known as kivas, which were probably used for ceremonial purposes. Because the rooms did not have external doors, people could gain access to them only by ladders from the roof. The pueblo housed around 1,200 people, and because it was so large, it was almost certainly the administrative center of the whole area.

The ruins of Pueblo Bonito, one of the great cities of the Anasazi people, are located in Chaco Canyon, New Mexico.

As the building grew up the wall of the canyon, each story was set back from the one beneath it, and the roofs of the lower stories formed terraces on which cooking took place and craftwork was carried out.

The first recorded sighting of Pueblo Bonito by a European was in 1849 CE, when US Army Lieutenant James H. Simpson discovered the complex during a military expedition shortly after the land on which it stands had been annexed from Mexico. When the site was fully excavated (between 1896 and 1900 CE), archaeologists discovered a series of petroglyphs (artistic rock carvings) depicting six-toed feet.

The Mississippians

Along the lower Mississippi River, another great North American culture rose and fell at around the same time as the Anasazi. That was the culture of the Mississippians, who built cities and towns around large earthen mounds—on top of which stood temples or the homes of the nobles and priests.

The largest of the Mississippian cities, Cahokia (near present-day St. Louis, Missouri), was home to ten thousand people at its peak and contained more than a hundred temple mounds, including one that was 100 feet (30 m) tall. Smaller satellite cities were built around the main city.

Like the Anasazi, the Mississippians grew vegetables and corn, and their reliable food supply meant that some of the people were released from toiling in the fields and were able to devote themselves to building temples and gaining skills in crafts such as pottery and jewelry making. Again, like the Anasazi, the Mississippian culture began to decline after around 1300 CE, and by the time the Europeans reached America, it had almost disappeared.

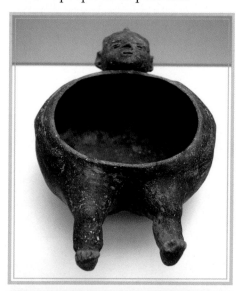

This ceramic bowl, found in present-day Tennessee, is a relic of the Mississippian culture.

Tribal Villages and Agriculture

With the disappearance of the Anasazi and Mississippian cultures, North America became a land of villages inhabited by tribes. A tribe might have thousands of members, but they rarely lived together in a single community. A very small tribe might have just one village, but most tribes lived in several villages scattered throughout their territory.

Tribes tended to be seminomadic. Those that relied on hunting or gathering wild plants for food kept moving in search of new supplies. Even when a tribe had learned to farm, it might still move around during the course of a year. It might have a summer village, where it planted and harvested crops, and then move to a winter village, which was better protected from bad weather or had a better supply of firewood. Some tribes had special hunting or fishing camps, where they stayed for several weeks during the spring or fall. A tribe might move around the same three or four locations every year for a generation or more. When the soil around a site was exhausted, or the supply of firewood was used up, the tribe would find another more suitable location.

When the members of a tribe moved from one location to another, they might leave their dwellings behind, or take part or all of them along. The tribes in the Northwest, for example, often spent the winter in substantial houses built of timber. When they moved to a hunting or fishing camp in the spring, they left their houses empty, taking their household property with them.

Other peoples left only part of their dwellings when they moved. Many tribes in eastern North America lived in **wigwams** (structures made from frameworks of poles covered with animal skins or mats made from grass). When those people moved on, they left the wooden frames, taking with them just the coverings. Other tribes lived in **tepees** (conical dwellings made from animal skins) that could be dismantled and reassembled in different locations.

Many villages were surrounded by fields of corn, beans, and squash. However, farming was not always possible. Much of Canada was too cold to raise crops, and the Great Plains were too dry. Along the Pacific Coast, on the other hand, food was so abundant that farming was unnecessary.

Along the Missouri River, a great deal of food came from agriculture. Farming was also important among the tribes of the Southwest, who inherited the Anasazis' skill with irrigation.

Farming was generally regarded as women's work. Men might help clear the fields and prepare them for sowing, but it was the women who raised the crops. The most important crops were corn and beans because they could be dried and stored for use during the winter. Many Native Americans also grew tobacco, which they smoked and used in their religious ceremonies.

Early Native American farmers did not keep herds of cattle, sheep, or any other animals, even after the Europeans introduced domesticated breeds in the sixteenth century CE. If they wanted to eat meat, they had to hunt or fish for it. The animals they killed also provided skins and furs that were used for clothing or as blankets for bedding. Hunting was men's work.

Clans and Family Life

In tribal villages, the people lived in family units. In some tribes, those units were nuclear families, consisting of a husband, a wife, and their children, all living together in a single dwelling. In other tribes, extended families lived together, either with several generations all living under one roof, or with a number of brothers or sisters living together with their spouses and children.

There were many different kinds of dwellings. As well as tepees and wigwams, dwellings included, for example, the Navajo hogan, which was a hut built of mud and logs. Extended families lived in larger dwellings such as longhouses, plank houses, and multi-room pueblos.

The Navajo of Arizona and New Mexico traditionally lived in hogans, or huts built from mud and logs.

In most tribes, individuals also belonged to a clan; among the Huron, for example, there were eight clans. In most cases, people were born into a clan to which they belonged for the rest of their life. Only in rare cases was it possible to change clans. Each clan functioned like an extended family, and its members thought of themselves as each other's relatives. They were expected to help each other and were often forbidden to marry members of their own clan.

Families and clans were responsible for many duties that would today be carried out by a central government. They were in charge of education, for example. Parents and older members of the family and the clan taught the young people the skills they needed to survive: hunting if they were boys, or farming if they were girls. Children also learned their tribe's customs: how to speak properly and behave politely, how to dress, and how to cut their hair. They were also taught the history of their family, clan, and tribe and their religious rituals. Such rituals marked the important stages of life. When a child became an adult, family and clan members conducted the necessary rituals, and when he or she married, the same people carried out the prenuptial negotiations. When a person died, the family and clan were responsible for ensuring that the person received a proper funeral and burial. In many tribes, the family and clan acted as the police and were responsible for punishing anyone who harmed or wronged another member.

The clan system played an important role in uniting the tribe by making individuals aware that they belonged to a larger social group than just a family or a village. A Huron of the Turtle clan, for example, could go to another Huron village and know that he would receive food and hospitality from other Turtle clan members in that village.

Languages

The members of a tribe were united by their language. Most tribes spoke a single language that was different from that of other tribes, although neighboring tribes often spoke closely related languages and could usually understand each other. Most tribes also had a name for themselves, names for other groups, and a clear sense of who belonged to which group. Some of the Native Americans known to outsiders as the Sioux, for example, call themselves Lakota, which means "allies" in their language. The word "Sioux" is actually a shortened version of a pejorative term applied to them by the Chippewa.

Religious Beliefs

Religion played an important part in uniting tribes. Many tribes had their own creation stories, in which their ancestors played a special role as the first human beings on earth. Members of a tribe often assembled at particular times of the year to perform religious ceremonies. They also gathered to hunt, go to war, hold tribal councils, or simply to celebrate their identity as a tribe.

Different religions were practiced by different tribes. Some of the religions were monotheistic (worshipping a single deity), while others had many gods. Some tribes had a recognized group of priests who carried out religious ceremonies, while other tribes believed that each individual was in charge of his or her own spiritual life.

Most tribal religions had several features in common, however. There was an underlying assumption that religion was an essential element in daily life; almost every human activity involved rituals that had to be performed properly in order to ensure success. Thousands of years ago, when hunting was still the principal source of food, the most important rituals involved animals such as bears and buffalo. Then, as more and more tribes learned to farm, agricultural rituals such as the corn and harvest festivals became important. By 1400 CE, many tribes both hunted and farmed, so both kinds of ceremonies were common throughout North America.

Kachina dolls, such as this representation of the Hopi war god, were both religious objects and toys for Native American children to play with.

Another common feature of most tribal religions was the belief that humans were just one of many species that shared the world with other living things and their spirits. Humans were no better or worse, they believed, than other animals. That did not mean that a hunter could not kill an animal, but he had to respect the animal's sacrifice and thank it with properly conducted rituals. If he did not do so, the animal's kin might feel insulted and refuse to cooperate in future hunts.

Tribal Leaders and Oratory

Native American tribes rarely had a single leader. Each village usually had its own leaders, whom the Europeans called chiefs. Some villages had just one chief, but many villages had two—one for leadership in wartime and the other for direction in peacetime. Some villages had one or two chiefs for each clan. Some chiefs were chosen for their hunting skills or their bravery in battle, while others inherited the position.

Native American chiefs were almost always men, but in some tribes, the chief was chosen by women or inherited his position through his mother's family. Regardless of how he gained his title, a chief usually had little real power. He could not force his fellow villagers to do anything; he had to persuade them to do what he wanted. For that reason, speechmaking was a vital and highly valued skill. When important decisions had to be made, the villagers gathered together and listened to speeches arguing for or against various possible courses of action. The speechmaking continued for as long as it took to reach agreement. The villagers never voted on a proposal because that would have left one side defeated and angry.

Conquests and Alliances

Sometimes, an especially powerful chief would gain control over several villages or even several tribes. His supremacy might be achieved through warfare or simply because he had a strong personality. Such empires were usually temporary, however, and rarely outlasted their creator. One of the most famous chiefs to gain control of an empire such as this was **Powhatan** (father of **Pocahontas**), whom European settlers encountered in Virginia in the early seventeenth century CE. Between

1575 and 1600 CE, Powhatan conquered several neighboring tribes and added them to his empire. He eventually controlled nearly thirty small tribes over which he appointed subchiefs. Powhatan made the conquered peoples pay tribute to him in the form of food or other goods.

Other tribes came together voluntarily. The Huron, Blackfeet, and Sioux all had voluntary unions of one kind or another. The most famous example of this type of cooperation was the League of the Iroquois, in the region that is now New York State. The league originally consisted of five tribes—Mohawk, Oneida, Onondaga, Cayuga, and Seneca. Those tribes had fought each other for many years before they came together around 1500 CE to end the fighting. A sixth tribe, the Tuscarora, joined the league around 1720 CE. Under the terms of the league, each tribe remained independent and made many decisions for itself, but an intertribal council was established at which all the chiefs met together to discuss issues that affected more than one tribe. This council allowed them to settle their differences peacefully, putting an end to fighting among themselves. Instead, they were able to devote their combined strength to fighting external enemies, which made the Iroquois very powerful.

Regional Differences

In spite of the many things that they had in common, Native Americans in different regions had quite different lifestyles. Tribes from the Iroquoian and Algonquian language groups lived in the Northeast and Midwest of what is now the United States. The former lived in longhouses, while the latter built wigwams; both peoples sometimes palisaded their villages (enclosed them within fences of wooden stakes). Their food came from farming, hunting, and fishing, and they moved between villages and camps in a regular cycle designed to take advantage of different resources.

In the Southeast, tribes obtained most of their food from farming (although they also hunted and fished), so they moved around during the year much less than the northern tribes did. Because of the warm climate, many tribes in the Southeast lived in open-sided houses. Their villages often included smaller versions of the great temple mounds previously built by the Mississippians. Some tribes also retained a social structure similar to that of the Mississippians, with a small class of nobles and a much larger class of commoners.

The tribes of the Pacific Northwest (modern Oregon, Washington, and British Columbia) developed some of the most elaborate societies in North America. They had a hereditary class structure consisting of nobles, commoners, and slaves. The temperate climate and abundant timber for building, together with the plentiful supplies of salmon in the rivers and seafood from the coast, provided them with the means and the time to build large plank houses, which they often decorated with totem poles that proclaimed the lineage of the inhabitants. Pacific tribes celebrated potlatch (winter festival) ceremonies in which people gained prestige by giving away their material possessions.

Most of Canada and Alaska was a subarctic forest with extensive bogs, lakes, and rivers and a harsh winter climate. Farming was impossible, and native peoples subsisted mainly by hunting and fishing. They were often nomads who followed the caribou herds on their annual migrations.

Farther north, along the Arctic fringe of North America, lived Aleuts and Inuits. Their ancestors were probably the last Asians to reach America and may have come by boat rather than over land. Most Aleuts and Inuits lived in small groups along the coast and survived by hunting whales and seals, although some hunted caribou inland. Both Aleuts and Inuits lived in igloos (houses built from blocks of ice), but they also built homes of turf and wood.

Native Americans living along the Missouri River belonged to farming tribes that spent most of the year in permanent villages consisting of circular earthen dwellings built on bluffs above the floodplain. They farmed the river valley (where annual floods renewed the soil's fertility), growing corn and beans, which were their staple foodstuffs. They also hunted buffalo on the Great Plains. They had no horses (horses were introduced by Europeans in the sixteenth century CE), so they hunted on foot. Their favored technique was to drive a herd of buffalo over a cliff and then kill those that were injured in the fall.

The desert regions of the Southwest were home to Native American tribes with two very different lifestyles. Settled agrarian tribes were composed of descendants of the Anasazi, such as the Pueblo, who, like their forebears, used irrigation to support their thriving agriculture.

Totem poles were a way for the native peoples of the Pacific Northwest to display and honor their tribal lineage. This totem pole features a bear and a raven, emblems of the Yaadaas clan of Alaska's Haida tribe.

They built large, permanent pueblos and developed an elaborate religion whose rituals were conducted in round underground structures known as kivas. Numerous nomadic tribes lived in other parts of the region. They subsisted either by raiding the settled agrarian tribes, as the Apache did, or by foraging in the desert for anything edible, which was the practice of the Paiute. Because wild food was scarce and took much time and effort to gather, these nomadic tribes were usually small.

The fertile coast of California was home to a greater number of different tribes (speaking a greater variety of languages) than any other region in North America. The area was so rich in resources that it supported a large population entirely without agriculture. Californian tribes did not establish permanent settlements but moved throughout the year, exploiting the abundant fish, game, and wild plants. The individual tribes were quite small, however, because the terrain (deep river valleys divided by rugged mountains) created many small environmental niches. Californian culture remained relatively simple because the people moved so frequently that they did not have the opportunity to develop more sophisticated forms of artistic expression.

A New Era

The arrival of the sixteenth century CE brought momentous changes for the native populations of North America. From the forests of the Northeast to the deserts of the Southwest, and from the shores of Florida to the snows of Labrador, tribes were making contact with European explorers for the first time. As settlers from Spain, England, and France began to colonize the New World, the Native Americans increasingly found themselves being displaced from their land and deprived of the natural resources they had once relied upon. Their cultures would never be the same.

Dating from thirteenth-century CE England, this map reflects the typical European medieval perception of the world, with Jerusalem at its center.

CHAPTER SIX

Europe Looks East

In the fourteenth century CE, Europeans had a very limited idea of the world, which they believed was centered on the holy city of Jerusalem and clustered mainly around the Mediterranean Sea. At the same time, however, they knew that, to the east, beyond the Muslim states that dominated western and central Asia, there were great civilizations in India and China. They knew that the steppes of central Asia extended for thousands of miles eastward and were the home of the **Mongols**. They also knew about Africa, which lay within sight of southern Spain, but they did not know how far that continent extended.

Missing from the European worldview was any concept of how the great land masses related to each other. It was not known what, if anything, lay beyond the Atlantic Ocean to the west of Europe, and it was generally thought that the majority of Earth's surface was land, rather than sea. In the fifteenth century CE, however, this began to change. The peoples of Europe entered a prolonged period of overseas exploration. These efforts led to the opening up of new trading routes and the establishment of colonies and settlements in far-flung parts of the world.

The Christian and Islamic Worlds

The Middle Ages saw the establishment of the concept of western Europe as "**Christendom**," with an identity separate from but linked to the Byzantine Empire (the continuation of the Roman Empire in the eastern Mediterranean and western Asia). The main external threat to Christendom came from Islam. Islamic armies had overrun much of western Asia, northern Africa, and Spain during the eighth century CE, and the relations between Christianity and Islam had been antagonistic ever since. Europeans launched a series of crusades (beginning in the eleventh century CE) to try to capture Jerusalem and other important Christian sites, but these military campaigns made no long-term gains, either in territory or in converts to the Christian faith.

During the fourteenth century CE, the Islamic world expanded into southeastern Europe as the Ottoman Turks conquered much of the Balkan Peninsula. In 1453 CE, the Ottomans captured Constantinople, the capital of the Christian Byzantine Empire. Although the empire itself had long been a mere shadow of its former self, the fall of Constantinople was of great symbolic importance to Europe.

There were many legends and fables about the lands that lay beyond the Islamic world. One legend concerned a Christian empire ruled by a monarch called **Prester John**. When Mongol armies attacked the Islamic world in the thirteenth century CE, many Christians in Europe hoped that the Mongols were under the control of Prester John. Even though this proved to be an illusion, European monarchs tried to form alliances with Mongol leaders, whom they saw as natural allies against the Muslims. Because of pressure from the successful Ottoman Turks, Europeans hoped they could find a way to engage the powers beyond the world of Islam to help them.

Trade with the East

Trade contacts provided knowledge about the world beyond the Islamic states of western and central Asia. Italian merchants such as **Marco Polo** (ca. 1254–1324 CE), who recorded his travels in a popular book, had visited and lived in some of the great civilizations of Asia because trade between eastern Asia and Europe was very profitable. In particular, spices (mainly cloves, nutmeg, and mace) from the **Spice Islands** (between Sulawesi and New Guinea in what is now Indonesia) were prized very highly in Europe. By the fourteenth century CE, there was a well-established trade route across the Indian Ocean terminating at Alexandria in Egypt. Merchants from Venice controlled the onward trade from Alexandria into Europe. The Venetians made enormous profits and jealously guarded their virtual monopoly.

Just as there were legends about unknown Christian kingdoms, there were also stories about the Spice Islands and the methods used there to harvest the spices. Many people had hopes that somehow, somewhere, there was a way around the route monopolized by the Venetians.

The difficulty with finding a way around the route controlled by Venice was that it was impossible to imagine an overland alternative. All land routes ran through territories controlled by hostile Islamic states. The only other option, a sea route, was barely conceivable for the medieval mind. One problem was technological. Medieval ships were not at all suited to long ocean voyages. Although Viking longships had crossed the Atlantic Ocean to Iceland, Greenland, and North America, next to nothing was known about these voyages in most of Europe. Viking longships were relatively seaworthy but could carry very little cargo. The ships that dominated warfare in the Mediterranean were galleys, which were unsuitable for the heavy seas of the Atlantic. With the development of trade in northern Europe, especially among the Hanseatic ports, larger vessels, known as cogs, had developed. Cogs could carry heavy cargoes, but they were slow and not very seaworthy. They could manage coastal trade in the Baltic Sea and the North Sea, but they found it difficult to cope with Atlantic swells.

A second problem with finding sea routes was that medieval Europeans did not have the necessary instruments to navigate out of sight of land. The compass, for example, only became available in the thirteenth century CE. Most navigation was carried out near land and was based on sailors' lore handed down from generation to generation, not on accurate measurements.

Finally, there was a psychological element, which lay in the mind-set that the center of the world was in the Mediterranean. Jerusalem and Rome were the foci of European cultural, religious, and political attitudes, and it was hard to think around that. The idea that Africa could be the home of prosperous, wealthy civilizations was difficult for the European mind to contemplate.

The Reconquista

The old preconceptions changed when one of the smaller European nations overcame the hurdles and helped create a new outlook for the whole continent. In the fifteenth century CE, the kingdom of Portugal was a thriving commercial and maritime country. Inhabiting a narrow strip of territory on the Atlantic coast of the Iberian Peninsula, the Portuguese were forced to turn to the sea, where they fished, whaled, and traded extensively with ports throughout northern Europe. They did particularly well trading in salt, and many Portuguese traders dreamed of being able to challenge the Venetian monopoly in the spice trade. The Iberian Peninsula had been one arena where the Christian-Muslim rivalry had been firmly decided in favor of Christian states. Islamic states had once ruled almost all of the peninsula, but a long series of wars known as the Reconquista had reduced the Islamic power base to a small enclave in the south, around the city of Granada.

The success of the Reconquista encouraged the Spanish and the Portuguese to contemplate the acquisition of further territories. They looked toward Africa and out into the Atlantic, and their expansionist spirit played an important part in the ensuing period.

Portuguese Expansion

One of the younger sons of the Portuguese king John I, Prince Henry (known as **Henry the Navigator**; 1394–1460 CE), became a pivotal figure in the history of exploration. In 1415 CE, the young prince took part in the conquest of Ceuta, a port on the northern tip of Morocco, and this triumph appeared to fuel a lifelong passion for exploration, both out into the Atlantic and especially down the coast of Africa.

As governor of Ceuta, Henry realized the extent of the trade between Morocco and sub-Saharan Africa. Gold and silver, rugs, spices, and slaves all came from the south, and Henry, together with other Portuguese nobles, realized the potential size and riches of the world beyond the Sahara. While at Ceuta, Henry began to sponsor voyages, and after his return to Portugal in 1418 CE, he devoted the rest of his life to pursuing his dream of finding a sea route around Africa and thus enabling Portuguese merchants to sail directly to the riches of the East. In 1419 CE, Henry established an academy at Sagres in southwestern Portugal and invited cartographers, navigators, and mariners from all over Europe to train young men (whom he called squires) to be maritime explorers.

Henry the Navigator, seen here, was a dedicated patron of maritime exploration, particularly along the western coast of Africa.

Henry linked this endeavor to his strong Christian faith. He became the formal administrator of a Christian order, the Order of Christ, in 1420 CE and was unusually ascetic in his personal life. However, Henry was also a successful businessman. He made sure that he profited from the voyages he sponsored. He acquired a monopoly on the supply of soap in Portugal and took over fishing rights; in 1433 CE, he was granted sole rights to the tuna caught off the Algarve. From the early 1440s CE, southbound expeditions began to bring back valuable cargoes, especially gold.

At first, Henry and his collaborators concentrated on creating a series of "stepping stones"—overseas possessions that would facilitate Portuguese maritime exploration. In 1420 CE, one of Henry's squires, João Gonçalves Zarco, claimed for Portugal the uninhabited island of Madeira. In 1427 CE, Portuguese mariners took possession of the Azores, a group of islands that later became a staging post for trade with the West Indies. Finally, in 1434 CE, on the fifteenth recorded attempt, a Portuguese ship rounded Cape Bojador, the most westerly point on the coast of Africa. The reefs and currents off the cape had defeated all previous expeditions.

Beginning in 1440 CE, Henry sent out yearly expeditions to push farther down the African coast. Cape Blanco was reached in 1441 CE, Cape Verde in 1445 CE, and the Cape Verde Islands in the following year. By the time of Henry's death in 1460 CE, Portuguese ships had reached as far south as present-day Sierra Leone.

Commercial rewards for all these endeavors soon followed. For centuries, there had been a thriving trade in African gold, which was brought from its source in the riverbeds of western Africa, northward

Navigational Tools

In the Middle Ages, oceangoing ships tended to hug the coastline so that their navigators could use landmarks to calculate their position. If a ship sailed out of sight of land, the navigator then had to rely on noting the position of the stars at night, combined with mathematical calculation. To help him in his calculations, he used two instruments—the **quadrant** and the **astrolabe**.

The quadrant was like a triangle with two long straight edges and a shorter, curved edge. A piece of string, weighted with lead, hung from the topmost angle. The navigator looked along one straight edge to take a sighting of either the sun or the Pole Star, and the weighted string showed the height of the heavenly body in degrees. To calculate the ship's position, the navigator compared his current reading with one taken in port before the voyage began.

The astrolabe was also used to take sightings of the sun and stars. The circular instrument was marked in degrees around its circumference. A sighting was taken with a movable sight bar, which then gave a reading in degrees. The astrolabe was easier to use than the quadrant because the quadrant's string would always swing lightly on a ship in motion, making it difficult to get an exact reading. The sight bar of the astrolabe did not have that problem.

Both the quadrant and the astrolabe could be used to calculate a ship's **latitude** (its angular distance to the north or south of the equator). To determine **longitude**, mariners used a system known as **dead reckoning**, in which they deduced their position from their direction of travel and the distance already covered. The latter was calculated by multiplying their speed by the length of time that they had been at sea.

The speed of the ship was measured with a rope that was knotted at regular intervals. One end was tied to a log, and the log was thrown overboard. An idea about how fast the ship was traveling could be gained from the speed with which the knots slipped over

This ornate astrolabe, made in France in the early fourteenth century CE, was used to determine a ship's latitude.

the side. That is why the speed of a ship is described in knots; one knot is equivalent to 0.869 miles per hour (1.6 kilometers per hour).

During the thirteenth century CE, the magnetic compass became a vital navigational aid. This instrument was developed by the Chinese, who discovered that if a spoon-shaped lodestone (a naturally magnetized rock) was placed on a board, the end would always turn toward the magnetic north. A crude compass was evolved by rubbing an iron needle with a lodestone to make it magnetic and then putting it in a straw floating in a bowl of water. Because the needle would always swing to point to the north, it provided a constant reference point for navigators.

across the Sahara Desert, and on to Mediterranean seaports such as Algiers and Tunis. Once the Portuguese had established forts and trading posts on the Guinea coast, they were able to tap into the gold trade at its source and bypass the Sahara Desert. The trade in gold was accompanied by a growing traffic in slaves. By 1448 CE, Portuguese trade had reached such proportions that Henry had a warehouse built on Arguin Island, off Cape Blanco, as a collection point and transit base for slaves and gold.

Henry did not accompany any of the expeditions himself; his importance lay in how he helped overcome the previous obstacles to European exploration by sea. His persistence in sponsoring voyages to the south eventually returned handsome profits. Most of the gains came from the sale of gold, but the crops grown by the colonists of Madeira and the Azores also made significant contributions to the balance sheet. In 1444 CE, the first privately sponsored expedition set off south with Henry's blessing. By the time of his death, exploration for profit had become an established practice.

Another of Henry's contributions to European expansion was his bringing together of groups of intellectuals to devise better ways of navigating at sea and to create better maps and charts (see sidebar, page 82). The Portuguese captains who led the expeditions were ordered to keep accurate logs, and their reports were closely analyzed. Mariners from other parts of Europe came to Sagres to learn and to impart their own knowledge. In the 1450s CE, Henry's expeditions often included vessels from other states. In 1456 CE, for example, the Venetian explorer Alvise Cadamosto headed an expedition in which there was also a Genoese captain (Antoniotto Usodimare) and one ship provided by Henry.

At a cartographical conference held in Florence in 1459 CE, delegates were shown a map that included information about the Indian Ocean and eastern Africa, and confirmed that there was a sea route around Africa to eastern Asia. When the Portuguese delegation returned to Lisbon to report its findings, a new wave of exploratory fervor swept the country.

Better Ships

The major advance during Henry's lifetime was in ship design. In the early fifteenth century CE, two types of vessels were developed that changed the nature of seafaring. These vessels were the **carrack** and the **caravel**. They combined elements taken from southern European ship design, from Arab dhows, and from northern European trading vessels. Both carracks and caravels were built around a rigid skeleton, and the planks that made up their hulls were butted against each other, rather than overlaid as in northern European vessels.

The carrack, developed from Mediterranean trading vessels, had a large stern that usually extended upward much higher than the rest of the ship and had plenty of room for provisions or trade goods. From northern Europe, the carrack adopted a large central rudder. Most previous European vessels had used just one or two square sails, but carracks were three- or four-masted. The mast nearest the stern carried a triangular lateen sail that gave the vessel enhanced ability to tack into the wind. Because they were big vessels, carracks were able to take on heavy ocean waves and could act as a stable platform for guns, something that was to have important consequences in the early sixteenth century CE.

The caravel was generally a smaller vessel than the carrack. Caravels carried two, three, or sometimes four masts, but the early vessels were generally just two-masted. These early caravels were usually furnished with lateen sails that gave them great maneuverability. Caravels had smaller stern castles than carracks and could deal better with shallow water, such as that near the reefs of Cape Bojador. Caravels quickly became an essential component of the fleets that Henry sent down the coast of Africa.

Rounding Africa

After Henry's death, King John II (ruled 1455–1495 CE) continued the quest for a sea route to the East. Having consolidated their position on the Guinea coast by the 1480s CE, the Portuguese mariners pushed on southward. In 1482 CE, one of Henry's former captains, Diogo Cão, reached the mouth of the Congo River. At that point, the Portuguese felt they might be on the brink of a breakthrough; the African coast veered eastward, suggesting that they had reached its southernmost point.

However, in the following year, Cão's hopes were dashed. On revisiting the Congo and exploring farther along the coast, he

Cartography

Medieval European mapmakers presented the world in a way that owed more to religion than to reality. They placed Jerusalem at the center of the world because of its religious significance.

However, during the crusades, Europeans came into contact with Arab scholars who had preserved knowledge from classical Greece and Rome that had been lost in Europe. In 1410 CE, one of the great works of antiquity was recovered from Arab sources and published in Constantinople. This work was the *Geography of Ptolemy* (ca. 90–168 CE), which summarized the state of knowledge about the world at that time and gave an accurate picture of the Roman Empire and its neighbors. In some respects, however, Ptolemy's account was wildly inaccurate. His world map showed Africa and Asia joined at the bottom, and, of course, he was unaware of the existence of North America and South America. Ptolemy's view of the world had an enduring influence on medieval mapmakers, and even his mistakes were taken seriously. Although Ptolemy knew that Earth was round, for example, he underestimated its circumference by around one-sixth.

The most accurate view of the world came from portolans (detailed charts made by Catalan fishermen and Italian mariners). The charts were of limited value, however, because they only recorded information with respect to coastlines.

The first modern atlases appeared in the sixteenth century CE. The Flemish cartographer Gerhard Kremer—better known as Mercator (1512–1594 CE)—developed a way of representing the spherical world accurately on a flat diagram. Mercator's projection is still important in cartography today.

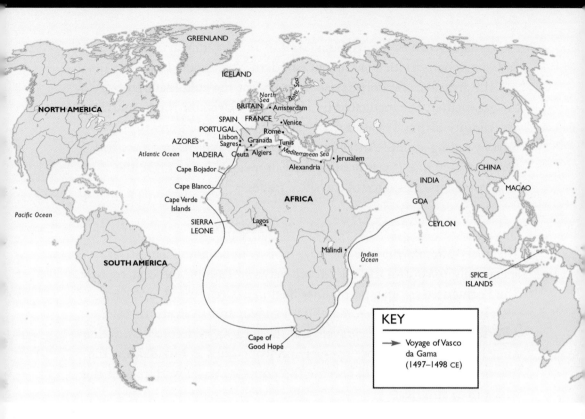

KEY

→ Voyage of Vasco da Gama (1497–1498 CE)

discovered that his ships were simply skirting a gulf; beyond it, the African coast again stretched southward, seemingly with no end.

The real breakthrough came in 1487 CE, when another Portuguese navigator, **Bartolomeu Dias** (1450–1500 CE), at last succeeded in rounding the southern tip of Africa. The weather was so bad that, at first, he failed to see the cape at all. Only after the storm had subsided did he find, to his intense joy, that the African coast had finally turned northeastward. He named the long, rocky promontory the Cape of Good Hope.

Internal difficulties and squabbles with their neighbor, Spain, prevented the Portuguese from following up this achievement for several years. It was not until 1497 CE that they mounted another major expedition, this one led by **Vasco da Gama** (ca. 1460–1524 CE). Commanding a fleet of four ships, da Gama followed Dias's route to the Cape of Good Hope, and then he proceeded up the east coast of Africa as far as Malindi (a port in present-day Kenya). There, he recruited a Muslim navigator, who piloted the Portuguese fleet across the Indian Ocean to the Malibar coast of India. On May 20, 1498 CE, da Gama's party landed at Calicut (modern Kozhikode, India).

The arrival of the Portuguese in India was the culmination of the great enterprise instigated by Henry the Navigator three-quarters of a century earlier. His idea that it might be possible to reach the East by sailing around Africa was proved right, and his mariners had demonstrated that it was feasible for European ships to make the long voyage to the source of the spice trade.

Building an Empire

The goal of the Portuguese was to establish an economic empire and, specifically, to control the spice trade between Europe and eastern Asia. The Portuguese set up a permanent fleet in eastern waters, and their vessels proved more than a match for Arab or Indian fleets. In 1502 CE, a Portuguese fleet of five caravels and three carracks defeated an Indian force by avoiding any close contact and firing guns in **broadsides**. The line of battle they adopted became the norm for naval warfare over the next three centuries.

The Portuguese concentrated on establishing coastal forts and depots from which they could conduct maritime trade. They built a string of forts along the east coast of Africa, and another on the shores of India and Ceylon (present-day Sri Lanka). On India's west coast, they established their main trading station at Goa in 1510 CE. Three years later, they reached the Spice Islands. They reached China in 1517 CE and later established a base at Macao. By 1520 CE, the Portuguese had laid the foundations of a trading empire that stretched from Africa to the East Indies.

However, the empire proved to be less profitable than the Portuguese government had anticipated. While Europe demanded Asian goods, the countries of Asia wanted little from Europe except for silver. The Portuguese were constantly challenged by European and Arab traders, and they never established a complete trade monopoly. Geography also counted against them. While their capital, Lisbon, was well situated for the sea route to Asia, it was poorly located for distributing spices to northern and central Europe. The Portuguese

Se Cathedral, in Goa, India, was built by the Portuguese in the sixteenth century CE. Today it is one of many architectural reminders of Portugal's colonial presence in southern and eastern Asia.

sold their goods to Dutch and Flemish merchants in Lisbon, losing out on the lucrative shipping trade up the west coast of Europe.

After less than a century, Portugal's dominance of the trade market with eastern Asia became jeopardized. In the 1600s CE, the Dutch capital of Amsterdam emerged as the principle port city of western Europe. This was largely the result of a northward power shift as Britain and France replaced Spain and the Italian states as the principal bankers of Europe. Money flooded into Holland, and the demand for exotic goods and spices rose. Dutch trade ships increasingly bypassed Lisbon, sailing directly to the Spice Islands and back to Amsterdam.

This sixteenth-century CE manuscript shows Amerigo Vespucci navigating by the stars. Inspired by Vespucci's account of the Brazilian coast, Martin Waldseemüller applied the explorer's name to all of South America in his 1507 CE map, the first to show the new territory as a stand-alone continent.

CHAPTER SEVEN

Exploration and Colonization

While the Portuguese were methodically exploring the western coast of Africa, hoping to find an eastward sea route to Asia, the Genoese mariner Christopher Columbus (1451–1506 CE) had another idea in mind: he hoped to reach Asia by sailing to the west. Instead, he stumbled upon the islands of the Caribbean Sea, inadvertently opening Europe's eyes to the previously unknown continents of North and South America. While **Ferdinand Magellan** (1480–1521 CE) was eventually able to round the southern tip of South America and continue sailing west to Asia, it was the discovery of the New World that proved to be truly earthshaking, both for the Europeans who proceeded to colonize it, and for the native populations that were already living there.

The Voyages of Columbus

Columbus fell in love with seafaring at an early age and learned his mariner's skills the hard way, serving on small ships that sailed in rough seas under tough captains. In 1476 CE, his ship was sunk by pirates and he had to swim 6 miles (9.6 km) to shore with only an oar on which to support himself. He found himself on the Portuguese coast near Henry the Navigator's academy at Sagres. From there, he made his way to Lisbon, where his brother was a mapmaker.

Over the next few years, Columbus became obsessed with an idea of the world that was deeply flawed but that gripped him for the rest of his life. Like other people who were familiar with the work of the

Egyptian scientist Ptolemy (ca. 90–168 CE), Columbus subscribed to the increasingly popular view that Earth was round, not flat. However, Ptolemy had calculated the circumference of the globe to be much smaller than it actually was. As a result, Columbus reckoned that the **Indies** (a vague location that could mean China, Japan, or the Spice Islands) only lay around 3,000 miles (4,800 km) west of the Canary Islands. Based on this miscalculation, Columbus became convinced that it was possible to reach the Indies by sailing westward from Europe.

In 1484 CE, Columbus sought finance from John II, king of Portugal, for a voyage of exploration. The king's geographers regarded Columbus's proposal as preposterous and advised the king to turn it down. They believed that to reach the East by sailing westward would entail a voyage of more than 10,000 miles (16,000 km). Such a voyage without any means of reprovisioning was, they argued, beyond the range of even the most up-to-date ships.

Undeterred, Columbus spent the next few years lobbying the monarchs of Spain, France, England, and again Portugal to give him backing for what he called his "Enterprise of the Indies." Finally, in 1492 CE, Ferdinand and Isabella, the Spanish monarchs, agreed to back him. In August of that year, Columbus's flagship (the *Santa Maria*) and two smaller vessels (the *Niña* and the *Pinta*) headed west from Huelva (in southern Spain) to the Canary Islands. On September 6, 1492 CE, the three ships sailed out into the Atlantic Ocean.

For the next two weeks, the three ships sailed westward with the help of a following wind. Then the wind dropped, it rained, and the crews became unhappy about the length of the voyage. They threatened to mutiny if Columbus did not turn back, and he had to promise that he would do so if they did not sight land within three days.

In the early hours of October 12, the lookout on one of the ships suddenly shouted *"Tierra! Tierra!"* ("Land! Land!"). By noon, Columbus stepped ashore on an island that he named San Salvador (the Holy Savior). Planting the royal banner in the sand, he claimed the territory for Spain. The island (which is one of the Bahamas) was almost exactly as far west of the Canary Islands as Columbus believed the Indies to be. He was therefore convinced that he had reached the extreme fringe of the Indies, and he named the local inhabitants Indians.

This iconic portrait of Christopher Columbus was painted posthumously and may not be an accurate likeness.

From San Salvador, Columbus sailed to the northern coast of Cuba (which he mistook for the mainland of Asia) and then to another large island (which he believed to be part of Japan). He named this third island Hispaniola (meaning "the Spanish island") in honor of his Spanish **patrons**.

The *Santa Maria* ran aground off Hispaniola and was wrecked. Columbus took this as a sign from God that he was meant to head for home, and on January 16, 1493 CE, he set sail for Spain, leaving thirty-eight men behind on the island with weapons and provisions for a year. By March of 1493 CE, Columbus was back in Spain, where Isabella and Ferdinand received him with full honors.

Columbus made three more voyages to the Caribbean over the course of the next decade, during which time the Spanish established a permanent presence in Hispaniola. The colonists, however, were divided by internal factions and became embroiled in conflicts with the native population.

Columbus steadfastly refused to accept the mounting evidence that what he had stumbled on was not the Indies but a whole new continent. He went to his grave in 1506 CE still convinced that the Caribbean region lay close to Asia and that the wealth of the Indies was just a little farther westward.

Dividing the World

With Portugal poised to establish a power base in the Indies (which Portuguese sailors eventually reached by the easterly route via the Atlantic and Indian oceans) and Spain apparently closing in on the same region via a direct route westward, the papacy moved to head off territorial disputes between the two rival nations. In 1493 CE, Pope

Alexander VI (ruled 1492–1503 CE) drew an imaginary demarcation line from pole to pole down the middle of the Atlantic Ocean. He decreed that all new discoveries to the west of that line were reserved for Spain and that any lands discovered to the east of that line were to be assigned to Portugal. In the following year, the papal directive was formalized by the Treaty of Tordesillas, in which Portuguese and Spanish diplomats agreed that the line should run approximately 1,185 miles (1,896 km) west of the Cape Verde Islands.

The pope's intention had been to give the Spanish freedom in the newly discovered lands to the west, while leaving the Portuguese at liberty to proceed toward their goal of reaching the Indies by the eastern route. One of the problems with the Treaty of Tordesillas, however, was that it was based on an incomplete map of the world.

The practical limitations of the treaty started to become apparent after 1500 CE, when a storm blew a Portuguese expedition under the leadership of **Pedro Álvares Cabral** (ca. 1467–1520 CE) drastically off course as it sailed southward along the western coast of Africa. Cabral eventually made landfall on the previously undiscovered eastern coast of South America and claimed the land (modern Brazil) for Portugal.

Two years later, the Italian-born mariner Amerigo Vespucci (1454–1512 CE) followed up Cabral's discovery by exploring the Brazilian coast. In 1507 CE, the German geographer Martin Waldseemüller (ca. 1470–1521 CE) drew on Vespucci's account of his explorations and published a world map that was the first to show South America as a separate continent. Waldseemüller named the new continent America in honor of Vespucci. Later in the sixteenth century CE, the name was also applied to Columbus's discoveries, producing two new continents, North America and South America.

Magellan Reaches the Pacific

In 1519 CE, the Portuguese navigator Ferdinand Magellan (1480–1521 CE) persuaded the Spanish king Charles V that he could reach the Spice Islands (the modern Molucca Islands in Indonesia) by sailing westward from Europe. If he succeeded, he would further undermine the effectiveness of the Treaty of Tordesillas by demonstrating that the Spice Islands, which had previously been visited only by eastbound Portuguese, were in fact to the west of the treaty's line and were thus legitimately Spanish territories. Magellan believed that, by sailing south along the eastern coast of South America, he would be able to round the southern tip of the continent and gain access to the ocean on the western side of the American landmass.

Once Charles V agreed to finance the expedition, Magellan set sail from Spain with a fleet of five ships on September 20, 1519 CE. He first crossed the Atlantic Ocean and then turned south, skirting the coast of Brazil. However, the expedition was beset by mutiny on the ships; Magellan was forced to execute two of his captains. There was further delay when Magellan decided to spend the Southern Hemisphere winter in Patagonia. It was not until October of 1520 CE that Magellan's fleet finally reached the strait that now bears his name. It took the ships thirty-eight days to pick their way through 325 miles (520 km) of treacherous, squall-plagued rocks that made up the strait, but on November 28, 1520 CE, they broke out into a vast ocean. Magellan was so relieved by the relative calm of the uncharted water ahead that he named it the Pacific (peaceful) Ocean.

The remaining three vessels of Magellan's fleet (two had been lost in the strait) proceeded northward along the western coast of South America and then turned westward, anticipating a short voyage to the Spice Islands. In fact, Magellan (like Columbus before him) had seriously underestimated the circumference of Earth; the ships did not sight land for almost a hundred days. The crews began to suffer from **scurvy** (a disease caused by a lack of vitamin C, which is found in fresh fruits and vegetables), and food ran so short that they were reduced to eating sawdust, leather, and any rats that they could catch.

Eventually, on March 6, 1521 CE, Magellan made landfall in the Mariana Islands, more than 1,000 miles (1,600 km) to the north of the Spice Islands. After taking on fresh provisions, Magellan continued westward, reaching the Philippines. There, Magellan became embroiled in a clash between warring native peoples, and while attempting to cover his men's retreat, he was killed by a poisoned arrow.

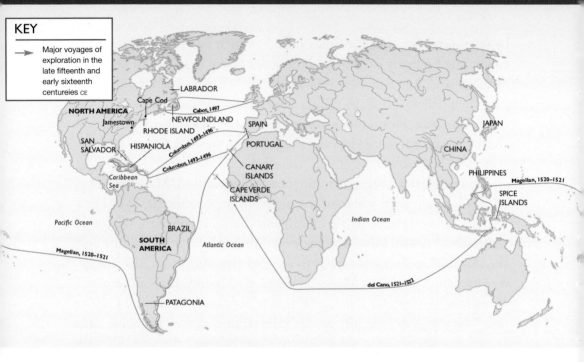

KEY

→ Major voyages of
exploration in the
late fifteenth and
early sixteenth
centureies CE

LABRADOR
Cape Cod
NORTH AMERICA
Jamestown
NEWFOUNDLAND
RHODE ISLAND
SAN
SALVADOR
HISPANIOLA
Columbus, 1493–1496
Columbus, 1493–1496
Caribbean
Sea
Cabot, 1497
SPAIN
PORTUGAL
CANARY
ISLANDS
CAPE VERDE
ISLANDS
JAPAN
CHINA
PHILIPPINES
Magellan, 1520–1521
SPICE
ISLANDS
Pacific Ocean
BRAZIL
SOUTH
AMERICA
Atlantic Ocean
Indian Ocean
Magellan, 1520–1521
del Cano, 1521–1522
PATAGONIA

Back to Spain

After Magellan's death, the surviving explorers, under the command
of Juan Sebastian del Cano, continued to search for the Spice Islands.
Only two ships from the original fleet remained, but they reached
Tidore in the Spice Islands in November of 1521 CE. One of the
ships, the *Trinidad*, then attempted to retrace the outward voyage back
across the Pacific, only to be captured by the Portuguese. The other,
the *Vittoria*, under the command of del Cano and laden with spices,
continued westward, crossing the Indian Ocean, rounding the Cape of
Good Hope at the southern tip of Africa, and finally reaching Seville
in Spain on September 9, 1522 CE. The ship had completed the first
circumnavigation of the globe. Of the 239 men who had embarked on
the expedition, only 17 returned.

    The success of Magellan's expedition was a remarkable achievement.
It demonstrated both the enormous extent of the Pacific Ocean (and
therefore the true circumference of the globe) and the fact that the
world's great oceans were connected. It did not, however, solve all
the mysteries of the world's geography. Navigators still dreamed of a
northern passage that would make the circumnavigation of the globe

easier than the dangerous southern route. Geographers began to wonder if there were any other continents to be discovered—perhaps a southern landmass in the vast Pacific Ocean.

Early North American Settlements

The discovery of the New World (as the American continent became known) transformed the European mind-set. The Old World suddenly seemed smaller, and the achievements of the great explorers whetted the appetite of ordinary Europeans for adventure and a chance to explore exciting new territories. The age of colonization was about to begin.

While Spain and Portugal established lucrative empires in Central America and South America, other European powers turned their attention to North America. Neither France nor England was successful in establishing a permanent foothold in the New World during the sixteenth century CE, although both nations made several attempts to do so.

In the early sixteenth century CE, the French made several expeditions to the New World. In 1523 CE, King Francis I of France commissioned the Italian-born sailor Giovanni da Verrazzano (1485–1528 CE) to find a sea passage through the Americas to the Indies. Verrazzano explored the eastern coast of North America, claiming everything along the way for France. Between 1534 and 1542 CE, the French explorer Jacques Cartier (1491–1557 CE) made three voyages to the mouth of the Saint Lawrence River in an attempt to find a northern passage to the Indies. On the last voyage, he brought settlers with him, but the small colony they established was abandoned in 1543 CE.

The first attempts by the English to make their mark on the New World were equally inauspicious. In 1584 CE, Queen Elizabeth I authorized **Walter Raleigh** (ca. 1554–1618 CE) to organize an expedition to settle the eastern coast of North America. An initial venture the same year landed on the coast of North Carolina and discovered native people who "lived after the manner of a golden age" and land that yielded "all things in abundance, without toil or labor." Raleigh named the new land Virginia, after the queen (who was known as the Virgin Queen). He sponsored two more voyages to the New

Northern Exploration

While some European explorers were intent on establishing colonies in the New World, others had not abandoned the hope of finding a northern passage to the Indies that would be quicker (or, at least, shorter) than the tortuous southern routes.

The first attempt to find a northern route was undertaken by the Genoese mariner John Cabot (ca. 1450–1499 CE), who set sail from Bristol, England, in 1497 CE in his tiny ship, the *Matthew*. He hoped to find a northwestern route to the Spice Islands, but his two-month voyage took him only as far as Newfoundland and Labrador, Canada. Cabot, who believed he had reached China, claimed the land for the sponsor of his voyage, the English king Henry VII.

In the sixteenth century CE, it was English explorers who were in the forefront of the search for a northwestern route. Martin Frobisher (ca. 1535–1594 CE) and John Davis (ca. 1550–1605 CE) both made several attempts to find such a route through Arctic waters. The mariners met and had dealings with the Inuit who lived in those inhospitable regions, but the expeditions were all ultimately defeated by pack ice and ice floes.

In the late sixteenth century CE, the Dutch looked for a northeastern route to the Indies—through the Arctic Ocean to the north of Russia. In 1594 CE, **Willem Barents** (ca. 1550–1597 CE) sailed up the coast of Norway and through the Arctic Ocean as far as the island of Novaya Zemlya, but there he found the way forward blocked by ice. Barents did not give up, even after a second failure. On his third attempt, he set a course due north of Norway and discovered the Spitsbergen Islands, where his ship was trapped and crushed by ice. Forced to overwinter on the ice, his crew built a house out of the timbers of their wrecked ship and caught seals, foxes, and bears for food. When the ice finally melted, in June of 1597 CE, the crew set sail in their longboats, but Barents died on June 19. The charts he made on the voyage were of lasting value to mariners.

It was not until 1903 CE that the Norwegian explorer Roald Amundsen (1872–1928 CE) became the first man to navigate successfully through the Northwest Passage.

This seventeenth-century CE illustration from an account of Willem Barents's voyages in the Arctic shows Barents and his crew stuck in the ice near the Spitsbergen Islands. They survived the winter by hunting polar bears and other native animals.

Today, the Jamestown historic site in Virginia presents a reconstruction of the first permanent British settlement in North America.

World (he never actually visited it himself) and attempted to establish a colony on Roanoke Island, off the coast of North Carolina. His expedition of 1585 CE was aborted after a clash with Native Americans, but the expedition of 1587 CE left around one hundred settlers on Roanoke. However, due to the outbreak of a war between England and Spain, supply ships from England were unable to reach Roanoke until 1590 CE. By that time, the infant colony had vanished without a trace.

At the beginning of the seventeenth century CE, a more successful attempt was made to establish a permanent English presence in the New World. In 1606 CE, a syndicate of English merchants was incorporated as the London Company and granted a royal license to establish a colony in Virginia. In April of 1607 CE, three ships carrying 104 English colonists reached the Chesapeake Bay, and the newcomers settled a promising site with woodland and fresh water several miles from the mouth of the James River.

The pioneer settlers of the Jamestown Colony—named for England's new king, James I (ruled 1603–1625 CE)—only just avoided the same fate as their predecessors had suffered at Roanoke. Although the colonists built a fort to protect themselves, along with simple cottages and a church, they had no defense against disease, particularly malaria, which swiftly reduced the settlement to around forty people. However, Jamestown survived under the resolute leadership of Captain John Smith (ca. 1580–1631 CE).

In 1609 CE, with the syndicate now reorganized and renamed the Virginia Company, some six hundred new settlers joined the few remaining original inhabitants of Jamestown. They, too, experienced dreadful hardships, and during their first winter in the New World (the so-called starving time), some 90 percent of them perished. They were so hungry that they reputedly dug up the bodies of the dead for food. The few survivors were on the point of abandoning the enterprise when relief ships arrived in the spring.

From this shaky start, the Jamestown Colony gradually established itself as the first permanent English settlement in North America. Progress was slow, but by 1619 CE, tobacco had been established as a successful cash crop, making Jamestown economically viable.

While the motivation behind the Jamestown Colony was primarily commercial, it was religion that inspired the next wave of settlement. In 1609 CE, a group of English Puritans who rejected the constraints of the Church of England emigrated to the Dutch town of Leiden, where their religion was tolerated. After a decade in Leiden, these so-called **Separatists** decided that only the New World would offer them complete freedom of worship.

The Separatists approached the Virginia Company, which was eager for new settlers and had no hesitation in granting them some land. In the fall of 1620 CE, some fifty Separatists embarked on the *Mayflower* at Plymouth, England, together with a similar number of other settlers, whom the "saints" (as the Separatists called themselves) described as "strangers."

The *Mayflower* made landfall at Cape Cod, far to the north of its allotted territory, and an advance party set out in search of a suitable site for settlement. They chose a spot that they named Plymouth, and, on December 26, 1620 CE, the passengers on the *Mayflower* disembarked at Plymouth Rock.

Before landing, the forty-one adult male settlers struck a deceptively simple agreement that would have a far-reaching effect

Pocahontas

Despite their tribulations, the first settlers in the Jamestown Colony were fortunate to have chosen a region where their intrusion did not provoke a determinedly hostile response from the Native Americans.

In this nineteenth-century CE engraving, Pocahontas intervenes with her father, Powhatan, in the execution of John Smith.

The local chieftain, Powhatan, ruled around thirty Algonquian tribes with an estimated total population of around ten thousand people. At first, the Native Americans chose to ignore the English settlers, but when food in the colony became scarce, Captain John Smith approached Powhatan's people with the intention of buying corn from them.

Instead of being welcomed, Smith was taken prisoner and brought before the chief, who condemned him to death. According to some accounts, Smith had already laid his head on the sacrificial stone when he was saved by Powhatan's thirteen-year-old daughter, Pocahontas. She flung herself down, covering Smith's head, and made an impassioned plea to her father to spare Smith's life.

Smith was saved, and Pocahontas befriended the settlers, helping to maintain peaceful relations between the colonists and the native peoples. However, after Smith left the colony to return to England in 1609 CE, the tribes became hostile again. In retaliation, the settlers captured Pocahontas, intending to use her as a hostage to obtain a lasting peace with Powhatan.

Pocahontas was well treated by the colonists during her captivity, and she converted to Christianity. Her father agreed to pay a ransom for her, but by that time, she had fallen in love with one of the settlers, the tobacco planter John Rolfe. She married him, and the marriage cemented general peaceable relations between Powhatan's people and the settlers during the critical early years of the colony.

on the political institutions of British North America and the future United States. Saints and strangers alike signed the Mayflower Compact, promising loyalty to each other and obedience to such laws as they enacted in their new home. In other words, they determined to govern themselves, almost like a corporation that granted equal status to all its members.

The local Native Americans played an important role in enabling the Plymouth Colony to survive. The Wampanoag tribe showed the settlers how to grow corn and squash, and how to hunt game. In the fall of 1621 CE, the settlers invited the Wampanoag to celebrate their first American harvest. The ensuing feast of wild turkeys and vegetables later became enshrined in the annual celebration of Thanksgiving.

The successful establishment of the Plymouth Colony was followed by a much larger influx of Puritans from England, where they were becoming increasingly separated from the established Church of England. From 1630 CE, English Puritans began settling the Massachusetts Bay area, and that wave of immigrants later became known as the Great Migration. Within a decade, an estimated twenty thousand English Puritans had immigrated to North America. The region in which they settled became known as New England.

Governor John Winthrop (1588–1649 CE) took great pride in his Massachusetts Bay Colony as an example of a model religious society. Eager to reinforce their faith, the Puritans punished dissenters harshly. Some of the inhabitants moved away to escape the strict government and established breakaway settlements in Rhode Island and Connecticut; towns also developed in what later became known as New Hampshire and Maine. By the 1640s CE, scarcely a generation after the Mayflower had landed at Plymouth Rock, the political and social structures of New England had developed into forms that are similar to those that exist today.

This fourteenth-century CE painting of Thomas Aquinas (*center*) encapsulates the Scholastic attempt to blend classical learning and contemporary Christian doctrine. Aquinas is flanked by ancient philosophers Aristotle (*left*) and Plato (*right*) while above him are Christ, the gospel writers, and other Christian figureheads.

CHAPTER EIGHT

Learning in the Middle Ages

I n the twelfth century CE, there was a revival in learning and the arts in Europe. During this period—sometimes known as the High Middle Ages—universities were established in many urban centers, particularly in Italy, France, and England. These houses of learning initially subscribed to the tenets of **Scholasticism**, a method that sought to reconcile newly rediscovered works of ancient philosophy with Christian religious dogma. As time went on, Scholasticism was replaced by **humanism**, a doctrine that affirmed the individual worth of every person.

In the Early Middle Ages (ca. 500–1000 CE), education had been confined to the clergy and had taken place mainly in monasteries, although some enlightened secular rulers also founded schools at their palace courts. When, in the thirteenth century CE, the monastic orders of the Franciscans and the Dominicans were founded, the friars were drawn to the new universities (especially to the University of Paris), where they established schools for members of their order. Talented friar-scholars soon entered the universities to study for degrees in **theology**.

Several universities grew up around respected teachers. The first university in Europe was founded in Bologna, Italy, in 1088 CE and developed around Irnerius (ca. 1050–1125 CE), a native of that city who taught the law code of the Roman emperor Justinian I (ruled 527–565 CE). The development of the University of Paris owed more to the teacher Peter Abelard (1079–1144 CE) than to the cathedral school of Notre Dame, which was its headquarters. In England, students gathered at Oxford, particularly to learn from Roger Vacarius (ca. 1120–1200 CE), a former student at Bologna who became the first teacher of Roman law in England. Vacarius produced a nine-volume study of Justinian's legal code, and that study became established as a legal textbook.

By 1450 CE, there were more than sixty universities in Europe. One reason for their proliferation was that, as royal government of centralized states became established, monarchs wanted educated administrators. Another reason was that the growth of trade led to the establishment of merchant companies and banking houses that needed literate staff. Lawyers were in demand, particularly as a result of the struggles for dominance between the papacy and Europe's secular rulers; their quarrels over the rights and privileges of each side hinged on the interpretation of the law and were often settled by precedent (taking arguments from ancient authorities and basing new verdicts on old legal decisions).

The Life of a Student

Students began attending universities at the age of around fourteen or fifteen. There were no examinations prior to entrance; any free man who was able to pay the fees could join. In the early days, many of the students lodged in private houses, hospices, or travelers' houses run by townspeople; two students commonly shared a room, and sometimes even a bed, to save money. By the end of the thirteenth century CE, because scholars often proved unruly and were prone to riot, most universities had built halls of residence in which they could keep students under closer supervision.

At the English universities of Oxford and Cambridge, living in the residence halls was compulsory. Students' rooms were cold, were seldom fitted with fireplaces, and often had wooden shutters in the windows rather than glass. The scholars took two daily meals together (dinner at 10:00 a.m. and supper at 6:00 p.m.), and they were required to dress as identically as possible at mealtimes. Rules were strict, and all kinds of contemporary pleasures were outlawed. Among the forbidden activities were keeping ferrets, hawks, or hunting dogs; playing musical instruments or singing; and playing dice or chess. Students had a curfew of 8:00 p.m. in winter and 9:00 p.m. in summer.

Grammar Schools

Before the rise of universities, education in Europe was traditionally provided by the monastic orders. In the twelfth century CE, around the same time that universities were being founded in European cities, monastic schools closed their classes to all except those wishing to become monks.

A new avenue of education was opened when the Catholic Church issued a requirement that all cathedrals provide an education in grammar. New establishments, known as **grammar schools**, formed the basis of a general growth in education. They were organized by groups such as merchant and trade guilds. Classes were open to secular pupils as well as to trainee priests. The subjects taught included Latin, theology, wool processing, navigation, agriculture, and medicine.

The spread of gammar schools was slow at first; by 1400 CE, there were only around forty grammar schools in England, but they proliferated during the Tudor period, particularly under Edward VI (ruled 1547–1553 CE) and Elizabeth I (ruled 1558–1603 CE).

In the Middle Ages, there were a few other sources of education. Parish priests provided informal schooling in the Christian faith. Some students attended schools for writing and singing. Literacy began to spread after printed books became more widely available in the sixteenth century CE.

Girls of any class had little access to formal education. Wealthy families sometimes provided tutors for their daughters, but the education given by those teachers focused primarily on household management and playing music—practical skills that could be of use to the women when they married and became homemakers. It was not until the sixteenth century CE that orders of nuns such as the Ursulines began to provide an elementary education for girls.

The University of Cambridge, in England, was founded by scholars from Oxford in 1209 CE.

The Liberal Arts

It took several years of study to qualify for a university degree. A course in the liberal arts led to a first degree, the bachelor of arts, after four or five years. There was no written final examination; students had to go through an oral test, known as the disputation, in which they answered questions posed by their tutors.

The arts course had two parts: the quadrivium and the trivium. The quadrivium comprised four elements: mathematics, geometry, astronomy, and music. The three-part trivium covered rhetoric, logic, and grammar. The trivium was the more important part of the course, and all the subjects it covered were taught from a Christian viewpoint with reference to the Bible and the works of the church fathers. A student who passed the disputation and was awarded a bachelor of arts degree was required to teach for two years before proceeding to three further years of study to gain a master of arts degree.

Group discussion played a central part in learning. Before the development of printing, books had to be copied by hand, and even university libraries did not have large collections of books. A good memory, a quick intelligence in debate, and the ability to construct arguments skillfully on the spot were essential for success. If books were used, the tutor would generally have the only copy and read aloud from it before beginning the group discussion; occasionally, the scholars would have one or two books to share among themselves.

Europe's universities formed an international community. Because Latin was the language of instruction and written scholarship, people from all parts of Christendom could communicate with each other, regardless of their native tongues. Scholars who could afford to travel moved freely from one university to another. Freedom of thought was less common, however. Church authorities oversaw all teaching and had the power to punish teachers who strayed out of line. In general, the clergy and most scholars agreed that the function of university education was not to discover new knowledge or to cast a fresh light on the world but to transmit established truths—the doctrines of the Roman Catholic Church—to the next generation. By and large, students were expected to absorb and pass on knowledge without questioning it.

Scholasticism

The ecclesiastical scholars who passed on the doctrines of the Roman Catholic Church to scholars at universities across Europe were known as Schoolmen, and their method of imparting information was called Scholasticism (from the Latin *scholasticus*, meaning "the product or property of the school"). Historians generally date the period of Scholasticism to the years 1100–1500 CE.

The Scholastic method attempted to reconcile opposing or apparently contradictory propositions by dialectic reasoning, which places in opposition propositions (theses) and counterpropositions (antitheses) with the aim of discovering the truth either in one of the two propositions or else in a combination of the two (synthesis). Scholasticism arose in large part as a means of reconciling the doctrines of the church with the thoughts of the Greek philosopher Aristotle (384–322 BCE), whose writings had recently been rediscovered in Europe through Arabic translations. Aristotle lived more than three centuries before the establishment of the Christian faith, at a time when people believed in a multitude of deities rather than a single god. He wrote on almost every aspect of human thought, including politics and science, but he did so without reference to a supreme supernatural being. His work, which stressed the importance of empirical observation and human reason or logic in understanding the world, was at odds with the implicit faith in God on which medieval Christian theology depended.

Christian scholars could not ignore the work of Aristotle. The rediscovery of Aristotle's texts had made the author widely known in Europe, and he was also respected in the Islamic world as a philosopher and scholar. The Schoolmen devoted their energies to solving the problems presented by the fact that such a great thinker had been able to interpret the world without reference to God.

Thomas Aquinas

The greatest of the Scholastic scholars was **Thomas Aquinas** (1225–1274 CE), a Dominican philosopher and theologian from Naples who took a master's degree at the University of Paris and lectured widely. His greatest work, the *Summa Theologiae* (*Summary of Theology*), was an attempt to summarize the Christian view of the world. Aquinas began the *Summa Theologiae* in 1266 CE, but it remained unfinished at his death. He is reputed to have abandoned it after undergoing a mystical experience.

Aquinas agreed with some of Aristotle's opinions, such as that all ideas originated in the senses, and he tried to reconcile that opinion with the view that whatever proceeded from reason was compatible with faith in an all-knowing God. Aquinas's writings argued in favor of the correlation of sense, knowledge, reason, and faith.

After Aquinas, Schoolmen wrestled with the apparent contradiction between reason and faith. Some of their arguments became so abstract that they bore little relation to anything that ordinary people could understand; the Schoolmen reportedly had heated debates on matters such as how many angels could dance on the head of a pin. Eventually, the obscurity of Scholasticism provoked a reaction against it that inspired freer, less constrained thought. That reaction became known as humanism.

Rediscovering Ancient Learning

The sixth-century CE Roman law code of Justinian, taught by scholars such as Irnerius and Roger Vacarius, was one of several ancient Greek and Roman works that were rediscovered by European scholars in the Middle Ages. Among the others were the writings on mathematics and engineering by Euclid (flourished ca. 300 BCE), Archimedes (ca. 287–212 BCE), and Hero of Alexandria (ca. 10–70 CE). Ancient medicine was also represented in the texts of Hippocrates (ca. 460–377 BCE) and Galen (ca. 129–200 CE). That those works survived to be rediscovered in the Middle Ages is due to the scholarship of Muslim Arabs and Greek Christians of the Byzantine Empire.

When the Arabs conquered the lands of western Asia, they inherited the knowledge that had been preserved there since the ancient days of Greece. Under rulers such as the Abbasid caliphs of Baghdad Al-Mansur (ruled 754–775 CE) and Al-Mamun (ruled 813–833 CE), translators created Arabic versions of Greek texts. Those works, along with texts preserved by the Byzantine Empire of Constantinople, inspired medieval Europeans to explore what they called the Greek sciences.

Advancing the Sciences

Many ancient sources were carried to Europe by Byzantine Greek scholars who escaped the conquest of Constantinople by the Ottoman Turks in 1453 CE. Among those scholars was the former Latin Patriarch of Constantinople, Cardinal Basilius Bessarion (1403–1472 CE), a theologian, humanist, and book collector who settled in Italy, where he donated his vast library to the republic of Venice.

One of Bessarion's ambitions was to translate the *Almagest* of Ptolemy (90–168 CE) from Greek into Latin. The Almagest was an astronomical treatise that detailed Ptolemy's conception of the universe as a series of concentric spheres with Earth at its center. Bessarion did not finish the translation before his death, but it was completed by his colleagues, and its appearance in Latin provided a spur to scientific investigation of the universe—even though its theories were proved wrong in the sixteenth century CE by new discoveries about the actual behavior of heavenly bodies.

This fifteenth-century CE French manuscript depicts a human dissection in progress. Dissections such as these contributed to an improved understanding of anatomy in the later Middle Ages.

The physical sciences were not highly regarded at a time when theology dominated intellectual activity, but the ground was nevertheless prepared for later advances in science. In Paris, French philosopher Jean Buridan (1300–1358 CE) demonstrated the inadequacy of Aristotle's laws of motion and attempted to establish his own law of impetus. Buridan's preferred methods of observation and experimentation were those that future scientists would follow.

Meanwhile, knowledge of anatomy was developed by the dissection of human bodies. Other scientific endeavors of the time included the use of compasses and astrolabes to plot coastlines and the use of mathematical principles to design domes and arches. Some areas of medieval scientific study are now discredited. They include astrology, which attempted to determine the influence of planets and stars on human behavior, and alchemy, which pursued the twin goals of creating an elixir of life that could cure all known diseases and finding a way to transmute common metals into silver and gold.

Gutenberg and the Printing Press

Around 1450 CE came one of the shaping moments of Western civilization—the development of the printing press. Although sometimes described as an invention, printing had been known in China since the tenth century CE but had not been transmitted to the West; the necessary techniques were independently discovered in the West in the fifteenth century CE. Several people were developing the process at the same time, but credit for the important technological advance is given to the German **Johannes Gutenberg** (ca. 1390–1468 CE).

This Latin edition of the Bible was among the first books printed by Johannes Gutenberg in the 1450s CE.

Before the development of printing, all books were written by hand (usually with quill pens) on paper or vellum (calf or sheepskin) with inks that were very difficult to use. One kind of ink, made from soot, gum, and water, had to be stirred regularly to prevent it from hardening in the pot. The earliest form of printing was block printing, in which a craftsman carved a whole page on a block of wood, which was then inked and stamped onto the printing surface. Gutenberg's breakthrough involved printing on paper with moveable type, forming words from individual metal letters that could then be reused on other pages. He used an alloy of lead, tin, and antimony to cast durable letters that could be used again and again. Gutenberg also invented a new, more practical kind of ink based on oil paints; he adapted presses (machines used for making wine and paper) to create the printing press, which pressed the inked letters against paper.

Gutenberg set up his press in Mainz, Germany. Among the first books he printed with his new process were a Latin grammar, an encyclopedia, and an elaborate Latin Bible, usually known as the Gutenberg Bible.

The Emergence of Humanism

Although Gutenberg's invention made printing easier, books were still rare and expensive. Printers produced no more than two hundred copies of any work, and each book was usually sold as loose pages and bound for a specific customer. Covers were made of a precious fabric such as velvet, silk, or leather and often had elaborate metal clasps to keep them closed. Gutenberg and other early printers attracted clients who, while not scholars themselves, wished to amass libraries that reflected their wealth, status, and culture. Noblemen such as the princes of the Italian city-states collected valuable works, including many editions of ancient Roman and Greek works, and employed scholars to study them.

Those scholars were known as *umanisti* (humanists). The name comes from the Latin *studia humanitas*, an intellectual discipline (developed in the fifteenth century ce and based on the study of classical texts) that incorporated grammar, rhetoric, history, poetry, and moral philosophy. The humanists believed that people who were versed in the studia humanitas would realize their fullest potential and develop qualities such as compassion and understanding alongside good judgment, fortitude, and the ability to speak eloquently. They argued that such studies could provide the basis for civic and political fulfillment and that education of this kind should be provided not only for the young but also for those already in power. Humanist study and philosophy principally involved close reading of ancient works, especially those of the classical era, but also consideration of the present and the future.

Learning in the Vernacular

The development of printing propelled a major change in European ideas and literature. Before long, printed books became much more common. By 1500 CE, there were as many as nine million books in Europe, produced by printers established in major cities such as Rome, Paris, and Cologne. In Venice in 1501 CE, Aldus Manutius issued the first small, portable, relatively cheap books. More people wanted to own books, and Manutius printed as many as a thousand copies at a time. He specialized in translations of ancient Greek texts.

Printed books made it possible to spread new ideas faster and to a wider audience than ever before. Although the earliest books were in Latin, works soon appeared in the **vernacular languages** spoken by ordinary people (see sidebar, page 112–113).

Of the many books published in vernacular languages, the most important and influential was the Bible, copies of which appeared in large numbers by the beginning of the sixteenth century CE. There had been vernacular editions of the Bible before, but few copies had been in circulation. Now, with the spread of literacy and the production of more and cheaper books, increasing numbers of people were able to read the Bible for themselves rather than depend on priests for their understanding of the scriptures. That development had a profound significance during the Protestant Reformation. The religious reformer Martin Luther (1483–1546 CE), who himself translated the Bible into German, based the new Protestant faith on his own personal study of the word of God.

Humanism was rooted in a devotion to classical learning, but its scholars varied widely in their interests. Some studied only textual matters; others, skilled in rhetoric and the rules of composition, acted as secretaries to princes and councils, preparing public documents or speeches linking contemporary politics to classical antiquity. For example, when republican Florence was resisting an aristocratic takeover, humanists encouraged resistance by drawing parallels with republican Rome.

Members of the Platonic Academy in Florence favored the teachings of the fourth-century BCE Greek philosopher Plato over those of Aristotle, who was studied by the teachers of Scholasticism.

Vernacular Literature

In Europe during the fifteenth century CE, the majority of people worked the land. Neither they nor many of their social superiors in the nobility ever learned to read and write. The only educated class was the clergy, and even some priests were illiterate. Literate Europeans were in the minority, and they wrote and spoke in Latin, the language of the ancient Romans, which had been preserved in church services.

Although used by only a tiny elite, Latin was an international language; it transcended geographical and political barriers and was one of the key unifying factors in the collection of Christian European countries known as Christendom. However, Latin was not Europe's only language; in everyday life, people spoke their local vernacular languages, the close ancestors of modern English, French, German, Italian, Portuguese, and Spanish. In the twelfth to fourteenth centuries CE, parts of Europe had begun developing their own written vernaculars rather than using Latin. The chansons de geste (songs of great deeds), which celebrated the exploits of great knights, were written mainly in Old French, beginning in the twelfth century CE. The songs of love performed by Provençal troubadours and French trouvères (minstrels) were also written in forms of French. In the early fourteenth century CE, the Italian poet Dante Alighieri (1265–1321 CE) wrote his epic poem *The Divine Comedy* in Italian. In England, Geoffrey Chaucer (ca. 1342–1400 CE) wrote *The Canterbury Tales* in English. These works gave respectability to native tongues. Vernacular languages had the effect of undermining the unity of Christendom because they reinforced the cultural barriers between its component parts.

The development of printing in the fifteenth century CE and the circulation of cheap books in vernacular languages in the sixteenth century CE homogenized the vernacular languages. Before

This fifteenth-century CE painting shows Dante Alighieri holding a copy of *The Divine Comedy*. On the left is the mountain of Purgatory, as described in the second part of Dante's epic poem, and on the right is his home city of Florence.

the fifteenth century CE, there had been no standard language in most countries. Regional accents and dialects were much more pronounced than they are today, and the tiny minority of people who could write in the vernacular simply spelled words as they thought best. The spread of printed books in the vernacular brought standardization of spelling and grammar and started a breakdown of regional varieties of languages. Over the centuries, English people began to speak the language that was standard in London, French people adopted the dialect of Paris, and so on.

Machiavelli

Florentine patriot **Niccolò Machiavelli** (1469–1527 CE) gave expression to one humanist view of the world in his celebrated book *The Prince* (1523 CE). He declared that it was the duty of every ruler to gain power and hold on to it by whatever means were available. He added that rulers should instill fear in their subjects in order to command obedience. Machiavelli served in the government of Florence from 1498 to 1512 CE and wrote *The Prince* in an attempt to gain favor with Lorenzo de' Medici, who overthrew that government in 1513 CE.

The Prince displeased many of Machiavelli's contemporaries because it paid no attention to the accepted ideas that secular rulers were God's agents on earth and that they should behave in ways that would be judged favorably by the Almighty. Machiavelli defended himself against that charge by saying that he was describing the conduct he had observed, rather than attempting to present it as a model of ideal behavior. He wrote: "I have thought it best to represent things as they are in life, rather than as they are imagined."

In the view of Machiavelli, society was not based on a simple, single moral code that governed rulers and subjects alike. The author believed that politics and power had their own morality. He expressed no opinion about whether the double standard was desirable; he merely told the truth as he perceived it.

Machiavelli's ideas were very radical in the sixteenth century CE, but many people think they are still valid in the modern world of realpolitik, where powerful people sometimes do what they can, rather than what they should. Machiavelli's philosophy was a major strand of humanism, but it was by no means the only one. Humanism supported a rich and varied approach to the world.

The humanists adapted to Christian thought Plato's teaching that all truth and beauty in the world were pale reflections of the supreme truth and beauty that exist eternally; they argued that people should try to understand these universal forms through reason, even though their understanding could never be perfect.

The World in Transition

In the view of many historians, the emergence of humanism marks a critical stage in the transition from the medieval world to the modern world. The movement ushered in a new view of the world, centered on humanity rather than on God, and established a tradition of classical scholarship. By accumulating, translating, and studying the works of the ancient Greeks and Romans, the humanists created a bedrock of philosophical and scientific works that provided the foundation of Western thought for the following three centuries.

The spirit of humanism was felt in a wide range of activities. Mapmaking, for example, boomed. At about the same time as the Genoese Christopher Columbus (1451–1506 CE) was planning a voyage across the Atlantic Ocean, the Florentine mathematician and cosmographer Paolo Toscanelli (1397–1482 CE) was attempting to prove that such a voyage would be successful. Indeed, Columbus carried with him on his first voyage to the New World in 1492 CE a copy of a letter and map sent by Toscanelli to the royal court of Lisbon. Columbus was also inspired to make his journey by the ancient scholar Ptolemy's *Geography*, which had recently been reprinted.

Humanist Politics

Humanism was largely developed by laypeople, who were independent from universities and religious institutions. As the movement spread, humanists across Europe formed their own scholarly community, corresponding with and visiting each other to debate their ideas and expand their knowledge. Many humanists developed an international outlook. One of the greatest humanists, the Dutchman Desiderius Erasmus (ca. 1466–1536 CE), turned down an offer of citizenship from the city of Zurich in Switzerland, saying that he preferred to remain a citizen of the world.

This nineteenth-century CE engraving shows a meeting between the great humanist thinkers Thomas More and Erasmus Desiderius. A portrait of King Henry VIII looks on.

Humanist scholars were welcomed at royal courts, where rulers sought their advice or basked in their reflected glory. Close acquaintance with government led the humanists to speculate on politics and social organization. At the court of the English king Henry VIII (ruled 1509–1547 CE), Erasmus met and befriended Thomas More (1478–1535 CE), who was lord chancellor from 1529 to 1532 CE.

More and Erasmus both wrote satires to expose contemporary corruption in church and state. Erasmus's *In Praise of Folly*, written in 1509 CE, delivered a biting attack on bad government, as well as religious corruption and human vanity. More's *Utopia* (1516 CE) speculated about an imaginary place where society was governed by principles of religious tolerance and social cooperation in contrast to the societies of selfishness and greed that the author perceived in Christian Europe at the time.

Both *In Praise of Folly* and *Utopia* revealed deep concern for the lives of ordinary people and respect for the social and moral values of people living in community with each other. Both works also condemned the privileged life lived at royal courts and in the higher levels of the Roman

Catholic Church, which they depicted as being preoccupied with wealth, social status, and unnecessary displays of splendor.

In general, humanists argued that rulers should conduct their affairs of state for the benefit and welfare of their subjects. They believed that men and women could improve their own lot in life. According to humanist thinking, both sexes should take an active part in the life of their communities, as they had in the societies of ancient Greece and Rome. For the first time in many centuries, thinkers praised an active, balanced life in the world, rather than the withdrawn, contemplative life of the monk. For example, the humanist Niccolò Machiavelli (1469–1527 CE), author of *The Prince*, rejected Christian virtues such as meekness, humility, and charity, substituting the notion of practical virtue. In his view, the virtuous citizen was someone who wanted to get ahead in the world and was eager for the material blessings of life. He was a man of valor, who placed a high value on duty to the state, loyalty, and patriotism.

The very idea of citizenship—of personal loyalty to a particular state or country, rather than to, for example, the church—was still novel at the time. It began to take hold, however, as Europeans gradually abandoned the notion of Christendom as a unified cultural entity, moving instead toward a modern concept of Europe as a loose collection of separate nation-states.

The lavish decorations of the Sistine Chapel, part of the Vatican Palace, are a great achievement of the High Renaissance. Seen here are the contributions from Michelangelo: the ceiling, painted 1508–1512 CE, and the *Last Judgment*, which occupies the entire west wall, painted 1534–1541 CE.

CHAPTER NINE

A Rebirth of Culture

The term **Renaissance** (French for "rebirth") is used to describe a cultural movement that brought Europe out of the Middle Ages and up to the brink of modernity. The Renaissance began in Italy in the fourteenth century CE and spread throughout Europe over the next three hundred years. The period was marked by a rekindled interest in learning derived from ancient Greek and Roman writings; by important scientific advances; and, perhaps most of all, by magnificent works of painting, sculpture, literature, and music. This flourishing of the arts was sponsored by the Catholic Church in Rome and by wealthy monarchs and aristocrats throughout Europe.

The use of the word "Renaissance" has been criticized by historians who object to the practice of giving names to periods long after they have ended because it implies that history can be split into separate sections, whereas it is in fact a continuum. While the point is worthy of serious consideration, it is important to bear in mind that some people in what is now called the Renaissance did indeed believe that they were entering a new age, breaking with the recent medieval past, and forging a link back to classical times. Early in the fifteenth century CE, for example, the German cleric Nicholas of Cusa (1401–1464 CE) was already referring to the centuries between the fall of the western Roman Empire in the fifth century CE and his own time, nearly a millennium later, as the *media tempus* (Middle Ages), a label that later became standard. Moreover, the word "Renaissance" (or *rinascimento* in

Italian and *renacimiento* in Spanish) was used by some men of the arts and sciences to describe their own times.

Yet there are important ways in which the concept of the Renaissance remains problematic. The period certainly did not see a sudden transition from a "backward" Middle Ages to an enlightened era. The Italian city-states that supported many of the greatest artists, writers, and architects of the period were also bastions of superstition and intolerance. Punishment for wrongdoers was often harsh. Disease, unemployment, and poverty made the lives of most people miserable and short. Violence was endemic as states fought each other and nobles vied for power. In Rome, supporters of one baron who strayed into a part of the city dominated by another baron risked being attacked or murdered by rivals and having their bodies thrown into the Tiber River. Privilege, factionalism, and cronyism dominated politics, religion, and everyday life.

Florentine Humanism

The Italian city-state of Florence is often seen as a key center in the development of Renaissance patterns of thought and art, including the philosophy of humanism. For centuries, the Roman Catholic Church had taught people that the highest goal in life was to withdraw from material temptations in order to contemplate divine truths, but the Florentine humanists instead advocated taking an active part in the world. They argued that there was nothing wrong with having material ambitions and amassing riches. The humanists were, in origin, scholars hired by the great lords of Florence and other Italian city-states. Their name was derived from that of their program of study (in Latin, *studia humanitas*), which was based on classical texts and incorporated grammar, rhetoric, history, poetry, and moral philosophy. They emphasized the need for education in those subjects to prepare the sons of wealthy lords for an active life in the community.

The Medici Family and Private Patronage

Art in the medieval period was a public activity; stained-glass windows and biblical narratives painted on church walls were there for all to see. During the Renaissance, however, the cultivation of artistic taste by members of the wealthy elite became a much more private matter.

Periods of the Renaissance

Although there are no firm dates for the beginning or the end of the Renaissance, the term High Renaissance is used by historians to refer to the years of greatest achievement in the Renaissance, especially in Rome, between around 1450 and 1525 CE. The label Early Renaissance is used for the period before around 1450 CE in Italy, particularly Florence, but it is also applied to the less developed style that was prevalent in parts of northern Europe until as late as 1550 CE. The period after around 1525 CE in Italy is usually called the Late Renaissance.

The number of art objects found in the private homes of the rich was far greater in 1500 CE than it had been a century earlier.

The accumulation of wealth in Italy is a key reason why artistic creativity began to flourish there. Italy's princes, bankers, and elite merchants were eager to advertise their wealth and status by becoming patrons of artists and architects. In the fifteenth century CE, when printing was in its infancy and books were luxury artifacts, rich people began to assemble private libraries. Many of the rich people also vied to engage the services of the most renowned scholars.

The greatest patron of the Early Renaissance period was **Cosimo de' Medici** (1389–1464 CE), the head of the banking family that controlled Florence. Cosimo ruled the city in the mid-fifteenth century CE and helped make it a center of humanist learning and the arts. He was a patron of the architects **Filippo Brunelleschi** (1377–1446 CE), who designed Florence's domed cathedral, and Michelozzo (1396–1472 CE), who built Cosimo a superb palace in Florence (now called the Palazzo Medici-Riccardi). Cosimo also supported the sculptors Lorenzo Ghiberti (1378–1455 CE), who created the *Gates of*

Lorenzo Ghiberti created ten bronze panels for the *Gates of Paradise*, including this one, depicting the story of Abraham.

Paradise (the magnificent gilded bronze doors to the baptistry of the cathedral), and Donatello (ca. 1386–1466 CE), as well as the painters Fra Angelico (ca. 1395–1455 CE), Andrea del Castagno (ca. 1421–1457 CE), and Benozzo Gozzoli (ca. 1421–1497 CE).

Cosimo de' Medici's example was followed by his grandson, Lorenzo de' Medici (1449–1492 CE), who became ruler of Florence in 1469 CE. Lorenzo the Magnificent, as he became known, was a humanist poet (who wrote in the Tuscan dialect, rather than in Latin) and a collector of antique manuscripts and works of art. He supported the humanists Marsilio Ficino (1433–1499 CE) and Pico della Mirandola (1463–1494 CE) and the poet Politian (1454–1494 CE). He was also a patron of the artists Giuliano da Sangallo (ca. 1443–1516 CE), Sandro Botticelli (ca. 1445–1510 CE), and Andrea del Verrocchio (ca. 1435–1488 CE), as well as of **Michelangelo Buonarroti** (1475–1564 CE) and **Leonardo da Vinci** (1452–1519 CE), those immortal names of the Italian Renaissance.

The concept of a famous artist whose name would be remembered was itself new in the Renaissance period. In the medieval era, artists were regarded as skilled craftsmen, rather like carpenters or bricklayers. Few people knew, or much cared, which craftsmen had made a particular stained-glass window or church pew—or even who had designed the great cathedrals. In the Middle Ages, it did not matter who made art; what mattered was that it was made for the glory of God. In the Renaissance period, on the other hand, wealthy patrons began to seek enduring personal fame through their patronage. They did not simply wish to display their wealth during their own lifetimes; they wanted to be remembered after they died, and the patrons' interest in lasting fame came to be shared by the artists they hired.

The publication of Giorgio Vasari's *The Lives of the Artists* in 1550 CE played an important part in this shift by focusing attention on the architects and painters who created the great works of the Renaissance.

Resurrection of the Son of Theophilus by Tommaso Masaccio is one of the first paintings to use the technique of perspective to create an illusion of depth.

Inventing Perspective

The wealthy families of Florence paid artists to decorate their private chapels, which were built in alcoves off the side aisles of churches. The chapels gave the wealthy a chance to demonstrate both their piety and their status through the value of their decorations and ornaments. Artists painted either frescoes directly on the plaster of the walls or canvases and panels to hang on the walls, especially above the altar. Some of the greatest frescoes were painted for a family chapel in the Church of Santa Maria del Carmine in Florence in 1424 CE. The frescoes, painted by Masolino (1383–1447 CE) and Tommaso Masaccio (1401–1428 CE) for Felice Brancacci, a wealthy Florentine, heralded a profound change in religious art. Christian art of the Middle Ages, represented mainly

The Lives of the Artists

One of the most influential developments in the changing status of the artist in the fifteenth and sixteenth centuries CE was the publication in 1550 CE of *The Lives of the Artists* by painter and architect Giorgio Vasari (1511–1574 CE). Vasari's book—a collection of biographies of painters, sculptors, and architects—remains a key source of information about the personalities and working methods of Renaissance artists. It had an enduring and profound influence on the promotion and consolidation of the new attitude toward artists; no longer essentially anonymous craftsmen, artists were henceforth viewed as individuals touched with a remarkable and valuable gift. Ever since Vasari's publication of his book, the lives, thoughts, and personalities of creative artists have become accepted as essential reference material for anyone who is interested in their work.

The first edition of Vasari's book gave more prominence to architects than to painters, but for the second edition in 1568 CE, he altered the emphasis, assigning painting primacy among the creative arts.

Vasari's work as an art historian overshadows his considerable life as an architect and artist. Born near Florence, he enjoyed the patronage of the Medici family for much of his life. For them, Vasari painted fresco cycles in the Palazzo Vecchio in Florence and designed the city's Uffizi Palace.

The Lives of the Artists reflected the culture in which it was written, reiterating the common humanist view that the medieval period was a "dark age" that produced no cultural achievements of any note. Like his contemporaries, Vasari looked back to classical antiquity to find artistic ideals. His principal concern was to celebrate the revival of the classical arts in Tuscany, which he dated to the work of Giotto (ca. 1266–1337 CE). Giotto painted beautiful early cycles of frescoes, notably in the Scrovegni Chapel in Padua around 1305 CE. According to Vasari, Giotto "broke with Byzantine style and brought into being painting as we see it today." Giotto launched the artistic progression that culminated in the works of Michelangelo, the only living artist mentioned in the first edition of *The Lives of the Artists*.

in stained-glass windows or illuminated manuscripts, rarely depicted individual features in human figures and made no attempt to produce a three-dimensional effect; images thus appeared to be flat. However, in one of the frescoes in Santa Maria del Carmine entitled *Resurrection of the Son of Theophilus*, Masaccio attempted to give the picture an impression of spatial depth by painting the crowd of onlookers beneath a frame of large buildings to the rear and making the figures of proportionate size, giving a sense of three dimensions. Arranging a picture in such a way is called giving it **perspective**.

Perspective was carefully worked out by geometry, the study of shapes. The discovery of how to do this, attributed to Florentine architect Filippo Brunelleschi (1377–1446 CE), was one of the great breakthroughs in the history of art. The use of perspective remained central to all Western painting until the late nineteenth century CE.

Artistic Subjects

Renaissance artists used radical methods, such as perspective, but they did not significantly change the Christian emphasis of their subject matter; their paintings and sculptures still used biblical subjects. Leonardo da Vinci (1452–1519 CE), a representative artist of the time, created *The Last Supper* (depicting Christ's final meal before his arrest and crucifixion) in the form of a mural in the dining hall of the Church of Santa Maria delle Grazie in Milan for Duke Ludovico Sforza and his duchess, Beatrice d'Este, in 1495–1498 CE. Michelangelo carved a series of beautiful *Pietàs* (statues showing the Virgin Mary cradling the body of the crucified Christ in her arms), the most famous of which (carved in 1498–1499 CE) is in Saint Peter's Basilica in the Vatican. Michelangelo also created a monumental sculpture of David (slayer of Goliath and king of Israel) in 1501–1504 CE to stand outside the Palazzo della Signoria, the government building in Florence.

Alongside the continuing biblical tradition, however, were themes taken from classical antiquity. Raphael (1483–1520 CE), one of the finest High Renaissance artists, painted the huge fresco *The School of Athens* in praise of Greek learning and culture—with the philosophers Plato and Aristotle depicted against a background of majestic ancient Greek architecture. Artists also looked back to classical antiquity for

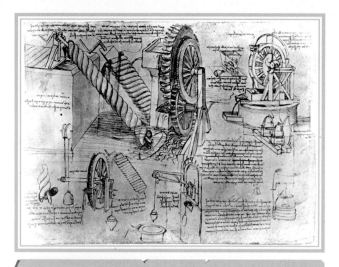

On this page from one of his many notebooks, Leonardo da Vinci sketched designs for various water-carrying devices.

technical inspiration. Michelangelo's statue of David, for example, recalls the style of ancient Greek sculpture.

Another development of artistic subject matter came about when powerful people began to have portraits painted in order to ensure that they would always be remembered by future generations. Leonardo da Vinci made a statue of his Milanese patron's father, Francesco Sforza, seated on horseback. Such equestrian statues, which showed men in a powerful pose, became fashionable. Carved tombs were another popular form of commemoration. Some patrons even had images of themselves and their prized possessions included in ostensibly religious paintings.

Papal Commissions

The most important patrons of the arts in Rome were the popes. Rome was a decaying city until Pope Martin V (ruled 1417–1431 CE) began rebuilding it, renewing its fortifications and repairing a number of its churches. The program of renewal was continued by his successors in the papacy, most notably by Julius II (ruled 1503–1513 CE).

Julius was the greatest of all the papal patrons. He commissioned the architect Donato Bramante (1444–1514 CE) to redesign Saint Peter's Basilica. Julius also commissioned Michelangelo to create his tomb and to paint the ceiling of the Sistine Chapel. In addition, Julius commissioned Raphael to paint a series of frescoes in the Vatican, a project that began in 1508 CE.

The Venetian Renaissance

Many Italian city-states made distinctive contributions to Renaissance art, and Venice was no exception. In fact, in the sixteenth century CE,

A Great Renaissance Man

Leonardo da Vinci, one of the most important figures of the Renaissance, is perhaps most famous as the creator of the haunting *Mona Lisa* (1503–1505 CE). He was also a man of extraordinarily wide abilities who left notebooks filled with remarkable designs, including a version of a helicopter and a military tank.

Leonardo represents the embodiment of the ideal Renaissance man, an individual who was learned in all areas of human knowledge and gifted in all types of human endeavor. Leonardo was both an artist and a military engineer. He was a scientist who dissected animals and noted the action of gravity, although he did not understand its cause. He anticipated that blood circulated in the body and envisioned machines that could fly.

Leonardo was born in 1452 CE in Vinci, a small town near Florence, and died in 1519 CE near Amboise, France; his life spans almost exactly the period known as the High Renaissance. From the age of fourteen, he was apprenticed to an artist and goldsmith, and by the age of twenty, he was one of the leading painters in Florence.

However, he was much more than a painter. When, at the age of twenty-nine, he applied for employment at the court of Duke Ludovico Sforza in Milan, he listed the accomplishments he thought would most appeal to a new ruler eager to establish himself in unstable times: the building of light, strong, fire-resistant bridges for the easy movement of troops; the invention of a device for removing water from military trenches; and the design of guns, mortars, and artillery-proof chariots (his tank). He also spoke of artistic achievements: "In time of peace I believe I can give perfect satisfaction and to the equal of any other in architecture and the composition of buildings public and private ... I can carry out sculpture in marble, bronze, or clay, and also I can do in painting whatever may be done as well as any other, be he who he may."

Leonardo da Vinci also worked in Rome, Bologna, and Venice, as well as in France, where he was given a home by the king.

Venice entered a golden age of painting, graced by such outstanding artists as Titian (ca. 1485–1576 CE), Giorgione (1476–1510 CE), Tintoretto (1518–1594 CE), and Veronese (1528–1588 CE).

Venice was also Italy's most important center for music. More than its rival city-states, Venice staged spectacular secular and religious festivals to mark the seasons of the year and the great events in the Christian calendar. Such celebrations usually included the performance of choral works in the cathedral of San Marco. Venice was home to **Claudio Monteverdi** (1567–1643 CE), often called the father of modern European music. Monteverdi wrote magnificent church music, including the exquisite *Vespro della Beata Virgine* (*Vespers of the Blessed Virgin Mary*) of 1610 CE. He also composed some of the earliest operas, and while most of them have been lost, those that did survive—*Orfeo* (first performed in 1607 CE) and *L'incoronazione di Poppea* (*The Coronation of Poppea*; first performed in 1642 CE)—are landmarks in the history of Western music.

Musical Advances

Music was traditionally written for the church, both for regular services and for special occasions. One outstanding Italian church composer was Giovanni Pierluigi da Palestrina (ca. 1525–1594 CE), who, in nearly a hundred masses, brought the tradition of **polyphonic** church music to its fullest expression. "Polyphonic" means "many voices," and polyphonic music has a number of separate melodic lines that are played and sung at the same time to create a shifting, harmonious combination. Palestrina's particular method for balancing and controlling these polyphonic lines was later codified by Johann Joseph Fux (ca. 1525–1594 CE) in a book that is still studied by composers today.

In addition to writing religious music, composers were increasingly turning their attention toward producing works for secular occasions, such as ballets and other entertainments performed at princely courts. The latter included several examples of the operatic form pioneered by Monteverdi and his fellow Italian composer Jacopo Peri (1561–1633 CE). Peri wrote an opera entitled *Dafne* (1597 CE), which is claimed to be the world's first fully fledged example of the genre, but it has been lost; his later *Euridice* (1600 CE) is considered to be the oldest surviving opera.

The most popular songs of the Renaissance period were **madrigals**, which were written for several voices (parts). In a madrigal, which is a polyphonic form, each voice follows its own melody while blending with the voices around it. Masters of the polyphonic style, such as Monteverdi and the Flemish composer Orlando di Lasso (1532–1594 CE), wrote hundreds of madrigals. Ranging in character from somber laments to lighthearted pastorals, these pieces became known for the madrigalisms, or witty musical devices intended to mimic the content of the madrigal's text—imitations of birdsong, battle sounds, laughter, or crying, for example.

The musical instruments that were most commonly employed from the early fourteenth century to the late sixteenth century CE were lutes and viols. Both are stringed instruments; lutes are plucked in much the same way as guitars are, while viols are played with a bow, like modern violins and cellos. Keyboard music, meanwhile, was written chiefly for the organ and the harpsichord, although the clavichord made its first appearance near the end of the period. The clavichord resembled the modern piano in that its strings were sounded by being struck with small hammers, rather than by being plucked in the manner of the strings in a harpsichord.

Like painters, musicians saw their status rise during the fifteenth century CE. The printing press, which helped with the spread of literature in vernacular languages, was also a great benefit to musical composers. Once their works could be published in printed form and performed in distant places, the composers themselves became celebrated figures in many countries. The printing of music also acted as a spur to the development and standardization of musical notation, the method of writing down exactly which musical notes performers should play or sing.

Beyond Italy

Italy was home to a great ferment of activity in the visual arts, but in music, the country was rivaled, if not eclipsed, by Flanders, a part of modern Belgium that was part of the duchy of Burgundy until 1477 CE (when it was annexed by France) and later became part of the Hapsburg Empire. Singers trained in Flemish cathedrals and in the churches of northern France were sought after throughout Europe. The Flemish composer Orlando di Lasso was born in Mons in Flanders, but thanks to his beautiful voice, he was taken into service by the viceroy of Sicily. He then prospered after finding favor with Duke Albrecht of Bavaria, in whose service he spent most of his adult life as a composer. For his contributions to church music, di Lasso was ennobled and made a Knight of the Golden Spur by Pope Gregory XIII in 1574 CE.

It was not only in music that northern Europe played a part in the Renaissance. Although the new styles in painting and architecture did not reach Germany, France, the Netherlands, and England until around a century after they had come to the fore in Italy, they had a profound influence when they did arrive. One of the first northern artists to feel the influence of the Italian Renaissance was the German Albrecht Dürer (1471–1528 CE), who made several visits to Italy. Possessed of an extraordinary talent for engraving and painting, Dürer produced traditional woodcuts on religious subjects, which allowed him to find the largest possible audience for his prints. He also painted panels and made woodcuts of secular subjects in a more modern, Renaissance manner. Dürer was one of the first artists in the world to practice self-portraiture, a form that would soon be firmly established by Rembrandt van Rijn (1606–1669 CE) in the seventeenth century CE.

In the Netherlands, the greatest pioneer of the new style in painting was the German-born artist Hans Holbein (ca. 1497–1543 CE), who was known for his precisely observed drawings and realistic portraits. In the early sixteenth century ce, Holbein painted highly individual portraits of King Henry VIII of England (ruled 1509–1547 CE), whom he served as court painter beginning in 1536 CE. Several Dutch and Flemish artists developed the tradition of painting biblical scenes in contemporary settings. Their works provide glimpses into daily life in the Low Countries in this era.

In France, the most lasting contributions to the Renaissance were the luxurious châteaus built during the reign of King Francis I (ruled 1515–1547 CE). Francis attracted many Italian artists and musicians to his court, and Italian and French architects and craftsmen combined to create the royal château at Fontainebleau. Although

The paintings of Pieter Bruegel the Elder (ca. 1525–1569 CE), including *The Census at Bethlehem*, are famous for placing biblical scenes in contemporary, everyday settings, a typical device of the Flemish Renaissance.

Renaissance French châteaus retained typical national architectural features, such as dormer windows and steep roofs, they also drew inspiration from the classical architecture of the Italian Renaissance. Thanks to printing, traveling artists, and the diffusion of culture by word of mouth, the new style of the Renaissance had in barely more than a century become prominent in many parts of Europe.

This seventeenth-century CE Japanese screen depicts a group of Portuguese traders arriving in Japan. The Portuguese first reached the island nation in 1542 CE.

CHAPTER TEN

The Passing of the Middle Ages

At the dawn of the sixteenth century CE, the world was on the threshold of great changes that were to have far-reaching effects on all humanity. Thanks to an accelerating program of exploration, conquest, and international trade, the ensuing hundred years saw more contact than ever before between disparate and previously isolated peoples. Some of the most momentous confrontations were those between technologically advanced societies and relatively primitive cultures who survived off the land and lived in ways that would have been familiar to humans fifty thousand years earlier.

Far-Flung Settlements

With the exception of Antarctica, there was human settlement on almost all the major landmasses by 1500 CE. The last substantial areas to be discovered and settled were the islands of the South Pacific Ocean, which were visited and then inhabited by Polynesian mariners, who crossed thousands of miles of sea in their outrigger canoes using observation and experience, rather than the navigational aids that were being used by European mariners. The last large area of the South Pacific to be settled was New Zealand, which Polynesians reached around the ninth century CE.

Even the most inhospitable of environments had been at least partly tamed by human ingenuity. The Arctic north was peopled by a culture that had learned to hunt marine mammals, such as seals, and make up for the lack of usable vegetation in that environment. Using snow and ice as building materials, and knowing how to endure the shocking cold, this culture was still expanding into new regions. In other cold northern climates, humans had developed methods of controlling and managing the vast reindeer herds of Siberia and Scandinavia, and they used the animals as the basis for a thriving society.

Over much of North America and the plains of South America, hunter-gatherers harnessed their natural resources so successfully that they did not need to form complex societies. On Tierra del Fuego, at the southern tip of South America, there was human activity based on hunting and fishing.

In arid regions, such as the Kalahari Desert in southern Africa or the desert interior of Australia, hunter-gatherers developed specialized skills that allowed them to use what nature provided and to identify sources of water from the slightest signs.

Even in the vast deserts of northern Africa and the Arabian Peninsula, human society had made its mark; Berbers and Bedouins used camels as the basis of a culture that had fierce resistance to outsiders but rigid rules of hospitality—two criteria that gave it identity and enabled a tribal way of life to prosper.

Tribes, States, and Dynasties

In lands where climatic conditions were favorable, farming and a settled agriculture had spread. In some areas—such as the region surrounding the Amazon River in South America, much of what is now the United States, large stretches of equatorial Africa, and what is now New Guinea—these agricultural societies had only rudimentary political institutions, which were little different from the tribal groupings of the hunter-gatherers.

However, over much of the world, agriculture had permitted the creation of larger and more sophisticated political institutions—states in more or less modern form. Societies of this type emerged independently in Japan, Korea, what is now Indonesia, Southeast Asia, China, the Indian subcontinent, western Asia, large parts of sub-Saharan Africa, northern Africa, Europe, Central America, and the western coast of South America.

On the great Eurasian steppes (to the north of the settled states of Asia and to the east of Europe) were societies of a completely different character; they were composed of nomadic peoples. From time to time, these nomads had successfully attacked the more settled societies. The most notable such events were the Mongol conquests of the fourteenth century CE. By the early sixteenth century CE, dynasties from nomadic tribes had become established as the Ottoman Empire in eastern Europe and western Asia, the Safavid Empire in Persia, and the **Mughal Empire** in India. The Ming dynasty in China was eventually overthrown by the Manchus from the eastern Asian steppes in 1644 CE. The struggle of settled agricultural communities against the steppe nomads was one of the constants of world history until technology gave the settled communities the edge in the nineteenth century CE.

Religion

Many of the world's states in 1500 CE were only just becoming aware of each other's existence—both the Americas and the southern tip of Africa were new discoveries for the Europeans. Nevertheless, despite having had no previous contact, many of these societies still had much in common. For example, they all followed religions that were sponsored by their respective states, although some were more tolerant than others of minority religions.

Martin Luther upended the Christian world when he started the Protestant Reformation in 1517 CE.

In some places, religion was barely distinguishable from the political apparatus. The conflict between religions, or conflicts in which religious differences played an important role, remained a centerpiece of world history for centuries, most notably in the confrontations between Christianity and Islam.

There were also schisms within religions that had far-reaching consequences. One was the division in the Christian church between the previously dominant Catholic faith and the reformed, or Protestant, variants that grew rapidly after 1517 CE, when the German monk Martin Luther led a movement to arrest what he regarded as the decadence of the established church. The other main example was the division of Islam into **Sunni** and **Shi'ite** sects. This division was particularly important because Persia had become a strongly Shi'ite state under the rule of the Safavid dynasty, and warfare between Safavids and Ottomans defined much of the history of western Asia for the next one hundred years.

Wars and Monarchs

Warfare was another defining factor of the states. It consumed a large part of the revenues that a state took from its peoples, drove technological change, and took on a momentum of its own (because warrior castes were often dominant politically). The causes of warfare were varied. In pre-Columbian Central America, the cause often seems to have been the need to take captives for sacrifice. In China, the Ming dynasty clearly tried to avoid warfare and, indeed, any contact with outside powers, but it was unable to do so. Warfare was part of the condition of statehood.

These states also had in common political structures that depended on a powerful single monarch. Even where the monarch had only a titular role, as was the case in Japan, there was generally another individual who wielded supreme power. There were, of course, elites that ruled countries and often had considerable local power and control, but most states depended on a single figurehead as a focal point for political stability. The problem of succession from one powerful single ruler to another was one that periodically convulsed many states. In the fifteenth and sixteenth centuries CE, the Hapsburg family averted possible conflicts over succession by voluntarily splitting their enormous European territories in order to make them more manageable.

Growing Cities

The emerging states often centered on towns and cities and sometimes on palace complexes. From Kyoto in Japan to Tenochtitlán in Mexico, the city was an important part of the state structure. Craftspeople,

This eighteenth-century CE illustration shows the arrival of Thai emissaries at the Forbidden City, the Chinese imperial palace in present-day Beijing.

traders, bureaucrats, and the members of the ruler's court all lived in urban surroundings.

The existence of these cities depended on the surpluses generated by agriculture. In nearly all states, other than a few small city-states, agriculture was still the occupation of the vast majority of the population, as it had been since the dawn of civilization. In spite of the social importance attached to eating meat and fish, the crops that kept societies functioning efficiently were wheat, oats, and barley in Europe and western Asia, and rice in China and southern Asia. Sorghum cultivation was critical in Africa, where the peasants who tilled the land were subjugated as part of complex social arrangements in which political control by a landowning aristocracy or by appointees of the ruler was supported by the hierarchy of the established religion.

International Trade

In the late fifteenth and early sixteenth centuries CE, improved methods of transportation and navigation brought previously isolated communities into contact for the first time. The famous voyages of mariners such as Christopher Columbus had blazed the trail, and armies followed in their wake to claim the newly discovered territories for the states of Europe.

Meanwhile, less spectacularly, international links were being forged through growing trade networks. The commodities being bought and sold were many and various; prominent among them were gold and other precious metals, furs, spices, and slaves. Some states became entirely dependent on trade in certain commodities. For example,

The Technology of War

The early sixteenth century CE was a period of technological change in warfare, and many of the encounters that took place during the period showed how important some of the innovations had become.

One of the most important military confrontations was between the Ottomans and the Safavids at the Battle of Chaldiran in 1514 CE. The Safavids had recently conquered much of what is now Iraq, but their army consisted of troops armed only with swords, spears, and bows. The Ottomans had both artillery and handheld gunpowder weapons, and they literally blew the Safavids away. Forced out of many of their recent conquests, the Safavids rapidly recruited and equipped their own infantry musketeers. Three years after Chaldiran, at Raydaniyya in Egypt, the Ottomans were again successful, this time against the well-equipped Mamluk cavalry. Because the Mamluks did not have artillery, Egypt fell to Ottoman forces.

Similarly, in Central America and South America, small Spanish forces were able to defeat much larger Aztec and Inca armies because of a technological advantage. Gunpowder was part of that advantage. In his siege of Tenochtitlán, Hernán Cortés used artillery to practically destroy the city before he took it. In addition to gunpowder, the Spanish had steel swords and defensive armor, whereas their enemies had no metal weapons. The Europeans were consequently unassailable. Stone missiles bounced off Spanish breastplates and helmets, while the slashing power of a steel sword was so great that one Spanish cavalryman boasted he had cut the hands off more than two hundred Inca warriors who had tried to stop him by grabbing at his bridle.

Songhai (on the Niger River in western Africa) successfully exploited the traffic of gold across the Sahara for hundreds of years, until Portuguese sailors moved down the coast of Africa and established ports that drew the trans-Saharan trade away from its historic overland routes. An important part of this emerging world trade was in textiles—silk and cotton from eastern Asia and wool from northern Europe.

Mighty Empires

In the early part of the sixteenth century CE, there were a number of large, or emerging, empires in the world. The Mughals were a Muslim people from central Asia. In 1526 CE, their leader, Babur, defeated the forces of the Delhi Sultanate near Panipat and then rapidly took over large portions of northern India. The Mughals continued to acquire territory in the region until the early eighteenth century CE, by which time they ruled almost all of what is now India and Pakistan.

In Persia, the Safavid dynasty came to power in 1501 CE, when Ismael I became the shah in Tabriz. The Safavids were originally a

The ornate architecture of the Iranian city of Isfahan, shown here in a nineteenth-century CE illustration, is a testament to the achievements of the Safavid dynasty, under which the city prospered.

religious order that used the military power of certain tribal groups as its military branch. The Safavids made Persia a Shi'ite state, and for the next two centuries imposed themselves on the different nomadic tribes that made up much of the indigenous population.

The Ottoman Empire was based in Constantinople, which the Ottoman Turks had stormed in 1453 CE. The Ottomans held sway in much of central Europe and, by the early sixteenth century CE, were increasingly influential in western Asia. They defeated the Safavids at the Battle of Chaldiran in 1514 CE and then defeated the Mamluk dynasty and took Egypt in 1517 CE. They extended their power along the shores of northern Africa as far as Morocco and continued to win victories in Europe. In 1526 CE, they shattered a European army at the Battle of Mohács and occupied Hungary. They soon controlled all the land around the Black Sea. The Ottomans also created a navy that allowed them to dominate the eastern Mediterranean Sea. The Ottoman Empire was the most successful state of its day, partly because it was relatively tolerant in religious matters, allowing its Christian and Jewish subjects to practice their own religions.

These three Islamic empires reached pinnacles of cultural achievement, especially in architecture and decoration. Cities such as Isfahan in Iran and buildings such as the Taj Mahal in India are glorious examples of Islamic art.

In China, the Ming dynasty had been established in 1368 CE, after a general revolt against the rule of the Mongols. By 1530 CE, China was the largest state in the world, with a burgeoning population of more than a hundred million people. It had a literate and efficient bureaucracy and was technically and scientifically effective. The Ming sent naval expeditions of huge seafaring junks throughout Southeast Asia, on two occasions reaching as far as the eastern coast of Africa (see sidebar, page 141). The Ming successfully defended themselves against invasions from the north, but they also discouraged foreign trade and foreign contacts; in 1522 CE, Portuguese traders were expelled from China.

This inward-looking policy of the Ming dynasty could not have been in greater contrast to what was happening on the Iberian Peninsula at the other end of the Eurasian landmass. There, the Spaniards, encouraged by the success of the Portuguese in finding a

Chinese Naval Exploration

In the early fifteenth century CE, the Chinese sent out a series of naval expeditions to assert their power overseas. Under the direction of Cheng Ho (Zheng He), a eunuch at the Ming imperial court, Chinese shipbuilders created enormous junks. In 1405 CE, the Chinese began using those junks in an unprecedented systematic exploration of Southeast Asia and the lands bordering the Indian Ocean.

This fifteenth-century CE Chinese manuscript shows the giraffe Cheng Ho imported from Africa.

Cheng Ho made a total of seven expeditions. On his first voyage, he was accompanied by around thirty thousand men and two hundred vessels. The fleet visited Vietnam, Thailand, Malacca, and Java. The Chinese accepted tribute from local rulers who greeted them hospitably and overthrew others who refused to pay homage. Cheng Ho's later voyages took the fleet beyond India as far as Hormuz on the Persian Gulf and eventually to Djofar and Aden on the Arabian coast. Cheng Ho then reached the eastern coast of Africa, where the Chinese captured a giraffe, which they took back to China for display in the zoo of the emperor.

All of Cheng Ho's voyages were part of a deliberate policy to expand Chinese power across the seas and to bring luxury goods into China. The Chinese began to regard overseas exploration as a waste of resources, however, and no further expeditions of this type were made. Even so, Cheng Ho's voyages established lasting cultural, trade, and immigration links between China and the countries bordering the Indian Ocean.

sea route to the Spice Islands, capitalized on Columbus's New World voyages to carve out an empire in the Americas. They conquered the Aztec and Mayan empires in Central America, and then in 1532 CE, a small band of Spanish adventurers under Francisco Pizarro overthrew the Inca Empire in Peru. Of all the natural riches in that region of South America, the most valuable was silver. That precious metal boosted the European economy and helped Spain to retain control of one of the world's greatest empires for hundreds of years.

European Colonies

The Spanish conquest and domination of the Americas was aided by two factors—disease and technology. Fatal European illnesses, especially smallpox, swept through American communities that had no resistance to them. Meanwhile, the Aztecs and Incas did not have steel, so Spanish armor and sharp-edged weapons gave the invaders an overwhelming advantage in hand-to-hand combat, while firearms and horses rendered the invaders almost unbeatable by indigenous peoples who had neither.

Perhaps Europe's most important technological advantage of all was the development of large, oceangoing vessels in the fifteenth century CE. Thanks to these sturdier ships, the open seas were no longer a barrier to European ambition. The sixteenth century CE thus saw the beginning of a great wave of international exploration, conquest, and trade. In 1522 CE, Ferdinand Magellan, on behalf of the Spanish, departed on the first expedition to successfully circumnavigate the globe. Within the next hundred years, the other nation-states of Europe—especially England, France, and Holland—would carve out their own far-reaching empires. They continued to exploit these overseas territories for centuries, with the help of the technological developments of the Industrial Revolution in the eighteenth and nineteenth centuries CE. While the United States broke free of its colonial status in 1776 CE, many of Europe's colonial holdings would not achieve independence until well into the twentieth century CE.

CHRONOLOGY

ca. 28,000 BCE
Hunters from Asia enter North America over land bridge between Siberia and Alaska.

ca. 17,000 BCE
First nomadic Asian hunters enter Central America.

ca. 10,000 BCE
End of last ice age; land bridge submerged by Bering Strait.

ca. 1500 BCE
Start of the Preclassic period of pre-Columbian history.

ca. 600 BCE
City of Teotihuacán emerges in Mexico; Iron Age arrives in northern Europe.

ca. 500 BCE
Zapotec people become powerful in southern Mexico.

ca. 300 BCE
Tiwanaku civilization begins to flourish in Andes. Start of the Classic period.

ca. 500 CE
Construction of Chichén Itzá commences.

ca. 750 CE
Teotihuacán destroyed by fire.

ca. 800 CE
Maya from Guatemalan lowlands move to highlands and into Yucatán Peninsula. Chimú kingdom becomes powerful on coast of Peru.

ca. 900 CE
Toltecs become major power in central and southern Mexico. Start of Postclassic period.

ca. 1000 CE
Chichén Itzá captured by Toltecs. Anasazi and Mississippian peoples emerge around this time. Leif Eriksson lands in America.

1088 CE
First European university founded at Bologna, Italy.

ca. 1100 CE
First Incas settle in Cuzco Valley.

ca. 1150 CE
Universities develop in Paris, France, and Oxford, England.

ca. 1200 CE
Nomadic Mexica people settle on Lake Texcoco, a region dominated by Tepanecs; Mexica later become known as the Aztecs. Anasazi complete major settlement, Pueblo Bonito.

1209 CE
University of Cambridge established in England.

1266 CE
Thomas Aquinas begins writing
Summa Theologiae.

ca. 1300 CE
Anasazi and Mississippian
peoples decline and disappear.

ca. 1321 CE
Dante Alighieri completes
The Divine Comedy.

ca. 1345 CE
Tenochtitlán and other Aztec
cities emerge.

1368 CE
Ming dynasty begins in China.

ca. 1400 CE
Aztecs oust Tepanecs as major
power in region. Three main cities
form triple alliance and subjugate
much of Central America.

1419 CE
Henry the Navigator founds
academy at Sagres, Portugal. In
the ensuing decades, Portuguese
navigators explore the western
coast of Africa.

1446 CE
Italian architect Filippo
Brunelleschi, pioneer of
perspective, dies.

ca. 1450 CE
First flowering of Italian High
Renaissance.

ca. 1452 CE
Leonardo da Vinci born.

1453 CE
Byzantine scholars flee to
western Europe after conquest of
Constantinople by Ottoman Turks.

ca. 1454 CE
Gutenberg Bible published
in Germany.

ca. 1458 CE
Aztecs conquer Mixtec cities.

1469 CE
Lorenzo the Magnificent becomes
ruler of Florence.

1479 CE
Aragon and Castile united by
Ferdinand and Isabella. Final
phase of Reconquista of Iberia.

1487 CE
Bartolomeu Dias rounds Africa's
Cape of Good Hope.

1492 CE
Christopher Columbus reaches
New World.

1493 CE
Huayna Capac becomes Inca
king; expands territory into
southern Andes.

1494 CE
Treaty of Tordesillas creates
north-south line in Atlantic

Ocean to provide boundary between regions of Portuguese and Spanish exploration.

1496 CE
Philip the Fair of Burgundy marries daughter of Spanish monarchs.

1497 CE
John Cabot sails from England to Canada.

1498 CE
Vasco da Gama reaches India by sea.

ca. 1500 CE
Pedro Álvares Cabral reaches South America. Five Indian nations form League of the Iroquois around this time; the Safavid dynasty is founded in Persia.

1503 CE
Julius II, great patron of Renaissance art, becomes Pope.

1505 CE
Leonardo da Vinci completes *Mona Lisa*.

1507 CE
Cartographer Martin Waldseemüller publishes the first world map to show a separate New World continent. He labels it America.

1509 CE
Humanist author Erasmus writes *In Praise of Folly*.

1514 CE
Ottomans defeat Safavids at Battle of Chaldiran.

1516 CE
Thomas More writes *Utopia*.

1517 CE
Protestant Reformation begins. Portuguese reach China via Atlantic and Indian oceans.

1519 CE
Spanish force under Hernán Cortés lands on east coast of Aztec Empire. Leonardo da Vinci dies.

1520 CE
Portuguese explorer Ferdinand Magellan rounds South America and becomes first European to enter Pacific Ocean.

1521 CE
Aztec forces overwhelmed by Spanish; up to half of all Aztecs killed by smallpox; end of Aztec Empire and culture.

1523 CE
Niccolò Machiavelli publishes *The Prince*.

1525 CE
Spanish forces conquer Maya in Guatemala. Epidemic kills half of Inca population.

1526 CE
Mughals overthrow Dehli Sultanate in India.

1528 CE
Albrecht Dürer, one of first artists of northern Renaissance, dies.

1530 CE
Coronation of Holy Roman emperor Charles V unites Burgundy, Spain, and German Empire under single ruler.

1531 CE
Chichén Itzá falls to Spanish explorers.

1532 CE
Spanish conquistador Francisco Pizarro conquers Inca Empire.

ca. 1540 CE
Pre-Columbian era ends.

1547 CE
Accession of Edward VI to English throne heralds increase in number of grammar schools.

1549 CE
Francis Xavier arrives in Japan.

1550 CE
Vasari's *The Lives of the Artists* published.

1584 CE
English make first attempt to colonize North America.

1597 CE
Willem Barents dies while exploring the Arctic Ocean.

ca. 1600 CE
Portuguese naval power declines; Dutch and Flemish maritime trade increases.

1607 CE
English establish Jamestown Colony in Virginia.

1620 CE
Mayflower takes first Puritans to North America; they settle in Massachusetts.

1643 CE
Italian composer Claudio Monteverdi dies.

1720 CE
Tuscarora join League of the Iroquois.

GLOSSARY

adobe Type of brick made from sunbaked mud and straw.

astrolabe Navigational device used by sailors to take sightings of the sun and stars for calculating latitude. The astrolabe was circular in shape and was marked in degrees around its circumference.

ayllu Administrative area within the Inca Empire.

Aztecs Mesoamerican people who controlled a large empire in central and southern Mexico from the fourteenth to the sixteenth century CE.

broadside Simultaneous discharge of all the guns on one side of a ship.

caravel Small, highly maneuverable, trading ship.

carrack Type of trading ship that was characterized by a large stern, a large central rudder, and three or more masts.

chaski Runners who were used to relay messages from one part of the Inca Empire to another. The runners were stationed at regular intervals along the empire's roads.

Christendom In the Middle Ages, the Christian world of western Europe. Defined in opposition to the Islamic empires of western Asia and northern Africa.

Classic period Period of American history that lasted roughly from 300 to 900 CE.

codex (plural: codices) Book made by the Aztecs and Maya; provided a largely pictorial record of their cultures.

conquistador Leader of the Spanish forces that conquered parts of Central America and South America in the sixteenth century CE.

dead reckoning System used by sailors to calculate the position of a ship in terms of longitude.

flower war War waged by the Aztecs specifically to capture people for sacrifice.

fresco Type of painting in which the paint is applied to wet plaster; usually decorated walls or ceilings.

grammar school Educational establishment that was open to secular pupils, as well as people training to be priests.

hieroglyphics Writing system that uses characters in the form of pictures.

huaca Sacred object worshipped by the Incas. Huacas could take the form of natural phenomena such as rocks, human-made objects, or mummified remains.

humanism School of thought that stressed the artistic, intellectual, and scientific achievements of humankind. With its secular outlook, humanism contrasted with earlier ways of looking at the world that centered around humanity's relationship with God.

Incas People who lived on the west coast of South America and ruled a vast empire that reached the height of its power in the fifteenth century CE. The empire stretched from present-day Ecuador in the north to central Chile in the south.

Indies Vague term used by people in the Middle Ages to describe a number of different places in Asia, including China, Japan, and the Spice Islands. Many of the great medieval explorers were trying to find a westbound route to the Indies.

Intiwatana Stone altar associated with Inca sun worship.

latitude Distance north or south of the equator; measured in degrees.

League of the Iroquois Confederation of tribes who lived in the northeast of the present-day United States. The league originally consisted of five tribes—the Mohawk, Oneida, Onondaga, Cayuga, and Seneca.

logogram Picture used to represent a word; used by Mesoamerican people such as the Olmecs.

longitude Distance of a place or object to the east or west of any given meridian; measured in degrees.

Machu Picchu Inca city located in the mountains 50 miles (80 km) northwest of Cuzco.

madrigal Type of song featuring a number of different voices; popular during the Renaissance.

Maya People who lived in present-day southern Mexico, Belize, and Guatemala. Their culture flourished between around 300 BCE and 1525 CE.

Mesoamerica Region of Central America, stretching roughly from present-day central Mexico in the north to Honduras in the south, that was home to a number of pre-Columbian cultures, including the Aztecs and the Maya.

Mixtecs Mesoamerican people who lived in the Oaxaca Valley from the tenth century CE.

Mongols Asian tribes of horsemen who originally came from lands to the north of China; were united by Genghis Khan in 1190 CE; and conquered central Asia, China, Russia, and the Delhi Sultanate in the twelfth and thirteenth centuries CE.

Mughal Empire Muslim dynasty that ruled India (1526–1857 CE); founded by Babur, a descendant of Genghis Khan.

New World European term for the Americas.

northern passage Northwestern route from Europe to Asia.

obsidian Type of glass formed by the cooling of molten lava. Mesoamerican people used obsidian to produce decorative objects, as well as tools and weapons.

Olmecs Mesoamerican people who lived on the coast of the Gulf of Mexico from around 1500 BCE.

patron Someone who commissions a work of art and pays for its production. Many of the great paintings and statues of the Renaissance were created under the patronage of the Italian nobility.

perspective Technique, developed in the Renaissance, that allows artists to create the illusion of three-dimensional space within their paintings.

polyphony The use of multiple simultaneous melodies in a piece of music.

Popol Vuh Mayan manuscript that is also known as the *Book of the Community*. The *Popol Vuh* contained the Mayans' account of the creation of the world.

Postclassic period Period of American history that lasted roughly from 900 to 1540 CE.

Preclassic period Period of American history that lasted roughly from 1500 BCE to 300 CE.

pre-Columbian People or a culture that existed in the Americas prior to the continents' discovery by Christopher

Columbus in 1492 CE. Often refers only to the peoples of Central and South America.

Prester John Mythical Christian ruler of an unspecified land in the East. Western nations hoped that he would join forces with them against the Mongols and the Muslims.

pueblo Housing complex made by the peoples of the southwestern United States. Pueblos were made out of stone and adobe bricks.

quadrant Device used by sailors to help calculate latitude. The quadrant was shaped like a triangle, with two straight edges and one curved edge.

Quetzalcoatl Major Aztec deity; represented as a feathered serpent. The Aztecs believed that Quetzalcoatl had appeared on Earth as a god-king and that he would one day return.

quipu Piece of knotted string used for administrative purposes in the Inca Empire.

Renaissance Period of European history marked by an increased interest in the works of classical writers, scientific advances, and a flourishing of the arts. Historians disagree about when the Renaissance started and ended, but it is generally agreed that the period was at its height between around 1450 and 1525 CE.

Scholasticism Philosophical movement that began in western Europe around 1100 CE; attempted to reconcile church doctrine with the teachings of certain Greek philosophers, particularly Aristotle.

scurvy Disease caused by a lack of vitamin C. Scurvy afflicted sailors on many voyages of exploration because of the lack of fresh fruits and vegetables in their diets.

secular Referring to the physical, rather than the spiritual, world; nonreligious.

Separatists Group of English Puritans who rejected the teachings of the Church of England and set up a colony in North America.

Shi'ites Supporters of Mohammed's son-in-law Ali; seceded from orthodox Islam after the murder of Hussein in 680 CE. Shi'ites (from shi'ah, Arabic for "partisan") believe that their leaders (imams) are divinely guided and have the right to Muslim leadership.

Spice Islands Islands in Indonesia; so called because they were the source of nutmeg, cloves, and mace; present-day Moluccas.

stelae Commemorative stone pillars.

Sunnis Orthodox Muslims who follow the Sunna (the body of Islamic custom).

Teotihuacán City in central Mexico that was the center of a large state by around 600 CE.

tepee Conical dwelling, made from animal skins, used by Native Americans.

theology Study of religion.

Tiwanaku Civilization that arose in the mountains of central Bolivia around 300 BCE.

tlatoani Head of the Aztec state.

Toltecs Mesoamerican people who built up an empire in central Mexico in the tenth and eleventh centuries CE.

vernacular languages Languages spoken by the ordinary people of a country, as opposed to the languages used by the clergy and other academics in writing (usually Latin).

wigwam Type of tent used by the original inhabitants of North America, consisting of a framework of poles covered by animal skins or by mats made from grass.

Zapotecs Mesoamerican people whose culture flourished from around 500 BCE to 500 CE.

MAJOR HISTORICAL FIGURES

Barents, Willem (ca. 1550–1597 CE) Dutch navigator who died while attempting to discover a northeastern route to the Indies.

Brunelleschi, Filippo (1377–1446 CE) Florentine architect who designed the dome of the city's cathedral; credited with the development of perspective.

Cabral, Pedro Álvares (ca. 1467–1520 CE) Portuguese navigator who, by chance, discovered the eastern coast of South America.

Columbus, Christopher (1451–1506 CE) Genoese mariner credited with being the first European to set foot in the Americas (although it is now established that Viking explorers did so several hundred years earlier).

Cortés, Hernán (1485–1547 CE) Spanish adventurer who led the force that brought down the Aztec Empire in 1521 CE.

Dias, Bartolomeu (1450–1500 CE) Portuguese mariner who was the first European to sail around the southern tip of Africa, which he named the Cape of Good Hope.

Gama, Vasco da (ca. 1460–1524 CE) Portuguese navigator who established an eastbound naval route from Europe to eastern Asia. He sailed around the southern tip of Africa and up the east coast as far as Kenya before crossing the Indian Ocean to reach Calicut.

Gutenberg, Johannes (ca. 1390–1468 CE) German inventor of the movable type printing press. He used the press to produce the Gutenberg Bible.

Henry the Navigator (1394–1460 CE) Portuguese monarch who sponsored a number of voyages of exploration.

Huayna Capac Inca monarch, ruled ca. 1493–1525 CE. During his reign, the empire reached its greatest extent.

Leonardo da Vinci (1452–1519 CE) Painter, sculptor, architect, and scientist who embodied the spirit of the Renaissance. His best-known paintings are the *Mona Lisa* and *The Last Supper*.

Machiavelli, Niccolò (1469–1527 CE) Florentine diplomat and writer. His most famous work is The Prince, a guide on how to succeed in politics.

Magellan, Ferdinand (1480–1521 CE) Portuguese navigator who began the first circumnavigation of the world.

Medici, Cosimo de' (1389–1464 CE) Florentine banker who was an important patron of the arts.

Michelangelo Buonarroti (1475–1564 CE) Italian painter, sculptor, and architect; responsible for the ceiling decorations of the Sistine Chapel.

Monteverdi, Claudio (1567–1643 CE) Venetian composer who played an important role in the development of the opera.

Montezuma II Aztec emperor between 1502 and 1520 CE; ruled at the time of the arrival of the Spanish conquistador Hernán Cortés; subsequently held captive by Cortés.

Pizarro, Francisco (ca. 1471–1541 CE) Spanish conquistador who led the forces that conquered the Inca Empire.

Pocahontas Daughter of the Native American chieftain Powhatan; saved the life of the English settler John Smith.

Polo, Marco (ca. 1254–1324 CE) Venetian merchant and traveler who reached China and met the Mongol emperor Kublai Khan.

Powhatan Native American chieftain who conquered and subsequently ruled over a number of tribes in present-day Virginia between around 1575 and 1600 CE.

Raleigh, Walter (ca. 1554–1618 CE) English adventurer who organized several expeditions to settle the eastern coast of North America.

Thomas Aquinas (1225–1274 CE) Scholastic philosopher and theologian. His best-known work is *Summa Theologiae* (*Summary of Theology*), which is a catalog of contemporary Christian thought.

FOR FURTHER INFORMATION

BOOKS

Bergreen, Laurence. *Over the Edge of the World: Magellan's Terrifying Circumnavigation of the Globe*. New York: HarperCollins, 2003.

D'Altroy, Terence N. *The Incas*. Malden, MA: Wiley-Blackwell, 2002.

Grizzard, Frank E., Jr., and D. Boyd Smith. *Jamestown Colony: A Political, Social, and Cultural History*. Santa Barbara, CA: ABC-CLIO, 2007.

Machiavelli, Niccolò (translated by George Bull). *The Prince*. New York: Penguin Books, 2005.

Man, John. *Gutenberg: How One Man Remade the World with Words*. New York: Wiley, 2002.

Sharer, Robert J., with Loa P. Traxler. *The Ancient Maya*. Stanford, CA: Stanford University Press 2006.

Townsend, Richard F. *The Aztecs*. London: Thames & Hudson, 2009.

Vasari, Giorgio (translated by Julia Conaway Bondanella and Peter Bondanella). *The Lives of the Artists*. Oxford, UK: Oxford University Press, 1998.

WEBSITES

Explorers
www.history.com/topics/exploration

Leonardo da Vinci's Notebook
www.bl.uk/turning-the-pages

National Museum of the American Indian
www.nmai.si.edu

Mesoamerican Codices
www.famsi.org/mayawriting/codices/index.html

Scholasticism and Humanism
www.philosophypages.com/hy/index.htm

Uffizi Gallery
www.uffizi.org